Life Happens

Even When You Are Standing Still

Dr. Ernest D. Lapierre

ISBN 979-8-218-91506-3

TABLE OF CONTENTS

DEDICATION

ACKNOWLEGEMENTS

PROLOGUE

ABOUT THE AUTHOR

DEDICATION

I dedicate my book to Arlton E. and Marjorie L. Lapierre, Prisciilla Cresswell, Penny, Peggy Sapphire, Monica Morrissey, Kristin Urie, and my family, especially my niece, Tracy Collier.

To my incredibly wonderful adoptive parents, Arlton E. and Marjorie L. Lapierre. While you may not have brought me into this world, you were everything to me, and you made it possible for me to exist in a world that brought many surprises. You never stopped me from doing anything I wanted to do, and even though you are not here with me in person, you are with me every step of the way in the creation of this book. This book is for you two very special people.

To my birth mother, Priscilla Caswell, who I never got an opportunity to speak with. Hopefully this book brings messages to you of how much I love you and how much I wish I could have met you. I wish you were here to share the joys of my life, among them the publication of my first book.

To my wonderful new friend, mentor, and unwavering supporter, whose presence I shall always treasure and strive to emulate for the rest of my life, Peggy Sapphire She was the person who listened to my ramblings on a Sunday afternoon in June this past year and then told me that I *had* to write a book about my life and that she would be glad to help me. How could I say no? Peggy, you were such an inspiration. I felt your warmth and direction. This book is for you, Peggy.

To my editor, Monica Morrissey, who took me on as a novice, a literal and figurative virgin in the field of authorship. If I had courage, you certainly had courage as well. Thank you for being there for me, especially when I most needed your presence.

To Kristin Urie, who put up with my constant *pestering* about what to do, where to find things like computers, and who else to seek for help. You brought me resources when I needed them. You have become an invaluable friend, mentor, and role model of what *giving back* truly means.

I would be remiss if I didn't dedicate my book to my wonderfully patient family, especially Tracy Collier and Penny Boyd, for their support and love through all the times I brought my past to the pages of today. You were always there in spirit and soul when those 2 AM awakenings came and it was time to get out of bed and work on my book. You were my best cheerleaders, keeping me going when times grew rough and I wanted to give up. Thank you from the bottom of my heart and soul.

To my readers, I don't think there are many things I wish I had never done, but there may be a few things I wish I had done differently or saved for another place and time.

ACKNOWLEDGEMENTS

I wrote this book hundreds of times in my mind and on my computer, only to hit the delete button and erase it or toss the pages I had written into the trash. I learned an invaluable lesson from this process: if you truly want to commit to something, tell one or one hundred people that you are going to write your book. Once you commit to someone else, you *will* write it, and you will not be able to back out.

I have so many people to acknowledge for their contributions to my success in writing and publishing this book. Without each and every one of you, I never could have completed it. Many thanks from the bottom of my heart.

Let me start with Lindsay Carroll. Thank you so much for your love and computer support when I thought I was losing it. Just the look on your face kept me going.

I want to acknowledge Jen Bushey for your constant support. Even when I thought I had drained every bit of support from you, you still had more to give. Your ideas and resources made the writing of this book possible.

Loriann Christie, what would I have done without you? You are my everything; from unceasing clinical care to suggesting a chair for my room that eased the pain in my back from working at the computer. Everything worked out because of you.

Joyce Hunter, my consummate supplier of paper; the very paper on which this book was written. Thank you for your steadfast supply and your wonderful support. I don't know where I would be without you.

Next, let me acknowledge my dining room table mates at the Craftsbury Community Care Center: Carolyn Miltner, Marsha Gadoury, Narcissa Gomes, and Donald Gray. Your support got me started and sustained me throughout the process. Thank you for your much-needed humor.

To every staff member and resident at the Craftsbury Community Care Center who met me in the hall and said, "So I heard you're writing a book," or, "What's your book about?I want to read it when it's done" I am so grateful. Your simple acknowledgement meant the world to me.

To Kimberly Roberge, our great administrator, for your wonderful smile that always let me know you were with me and brought me courage when I had been drained of my last drop.

To Jen and Joe Welker, whose steadfast love sustained me through the days and nights until I could finish this book, thank you.

To Linda Harder, who always checked in on me and my precious book, while putting in my hearing aids early every morning. Thank you for your presence and care.

Prologue

This book is written for anyone who is adopted and has considered finding their birth family, keeping in mind that this is a choice only *you* can make. Remember that if you ask the question, you must be ready for the answer. You may not always like the answer, but you will have to live with it. Don't be afraid. What if the person you reach out to says they do not want further contact? When I began seeking my birth family, I made it clear that I wished to talk with them and, if possible, meet them. And I made sure I had a support system in place in case the news I received was not what I had hoped for.

I decided to write this book as an open and honest autobiography with the hope that there were no taboos too great, and that you will find solace in my reflections and disclosures, and in turn feel encouraged to explore your own. It isn't always easy, but it is almost always worthwhile. Often, taking the road less traveled brings unexpected benefits. It certainly did for me. Courage is the operative word; with the realization that life often happens even when you do nothing more than stand still.

Growing up and encountering so many things I didn't understand, I often wished I had a resource, a book or a person, to whom I could turn with my questions. Someone who could tell me what to do or where to go when something went wrong. It would have been nice to have known about people, resources, or organizations that could have helped me find my way. I felt lost and alone at times, with no direction and no one to turn to. I often felt like I was stumbling in the dark. Was that feeling rooted in being taken from my birth mother as an infant, or was it something deeper within me? Did it include anger at my birth father, as though a wall crashed down when I realized he had abandoned me as well? I simply needed someone to tell me that I was going to be okay; that everything would turn out alright.

I needed courage and support to ask tough questions, such as what it meant to be a gay person. I was too afraid to ask anyone. I also needed an old-fashioned Julia Child–style cookbook that would say, "When one recipe fails, turn to page X and try recipe Y. But whatever you do, don't give up!" I avoided asking my parents questions because I feared they would say, "You don't know what you're talking about. You don't need to know that." I certainly didn't need to hear that. And what about seeing a psychiatrist to talk about my thoughts and feelings? Forget it. In that time period, it simply wasn't something you did, especially because we didn't have the money. Back then, seeing a psychiatrist was often perceived as airing your dirty laundry in front of strangers. Anything that I would have wanted to talk about was considered nobody's business but the family's.

I wrote this book to share my past, my present, and my hopes for the future, with the strong belief that I had to go through every good and bad experience to become who I am today. Some days, that still doesn't make sense. You will have to indulge me, because I love humor, and the pages of this book are sprinkled with moments of jocularity. I often speak to you as if we are sitting together, face to face. I find that it personalizes the experience, and I hope you will feel that, too.

These accounts are one person's version of the good, the bad, and the ugly. For example, I struggled with whether to include my experiences with sadomasochism because I was deeply embarrassed by them. But after much thought, just as with other difficult subjects, I realized I had to include them to remain honest with you, the reader. Honesty was my commitment, and now I am glad I stayed true to it. I am grateful to have had the opportunity to express myself in this deeply cathartic way.

About the Author

I am Ernie Lapierre, and I am 76 years old. I am retired now, living in Craftsbury, VT. I had a wonderful 51-year career in Nursing, from Registered Nurse to Advanced Practice Nurse in Private Practice in Adult Psychiatric Mental Health Nursing. In addition, I was a Nurse Researcher and Nurse Educator. I was honored to experience military nursing careers, serving as a Captain in the National Guard and as a Commander in the United States Public Health Service (USPHS). I received several honors in my life, including the Army Achievement Medal, which requires an act of Congress to receive, and recognition for Outstanding Service to the USPHS.

Among my hobbies, I enjoyed skiing, hiking, and bicycling. More than anything, I enjoyed playing the piano for my own pleasure as well as for the enjoyment of others. I liked solitary sports such as track and cross-country. I learned and enjoyed knitting, crocheting, and needlepoint. You might say that I truly enjoyed weaving the tapestry of my life into artistic works.

I have a myriad of life experiences: being adopted, growing up poor, leaving home right after high school graduation, becoming well-educated, often having to achieve things on my own, experiencing numerous jobs, having stints with the military, being gay, finding my birth family after 70 years of not knowing who or where they were, numerous health issues, and retiring after 51 years of work in Nursing. I was the author of several medical and nursing journal articles over the years and wrote a couple of chapters for nursing books as well. While you might say that being a Nurse Educator was a career, it was also a hobby because I often made it very creative.

One final reason I have for writing this book is something you will quickly learn about me: I am an empath. Being an empath gives me free license not only to experience the needs of others and myself, but also to meet them when possible. Being an empath is a character trait that allows me to write in the tone this book needed, which is exactly what this book is.

In a recent therapy session, my therapist asked me what I thought had made the change I was talking about because of how happy I had been lately. I answered that it happened when I realized I had choices, that life was not all cast in stone. I quickly recognized that one choice I had was *not* making a choice, and that freed me enough to gain composure of my own being and helped me in the authorship of this book.

I don't think it was any coincidence that since I started writing this book, I likened it to a jigsaw puzzle. There are two different jigsaw puzzles in two boxes. One box was my adopted family and the other box was my birth family. I think of life as very much like a jigsaw puzzle, where you usually start with the outer-edge pieces first, then work on the inside pieces next, until the puzzle is finished and you have the complete picture before you.

When I sat down with Peggy Saphirre that bleak Sunday afternoon in June of 2025, I thought the reason she had invited me was to share her story about her illustrious writing career, which I was fascinated by and ready to hear. Little did I know she had other things in mind for me. After a brief interlude about her writing career, we launched into a story about my life and all the things I had done. I couldn't believe how politely she sat. She was very still, smiling and laughing appropriately as I mentioned both jocular and serious moments of my life.

After we finished, Peggy looked at me seriously and said, "You know what you have to do now? You have to write your story." My jaw dropped to the floor because those were the last words I expected to hear from her. But I believed she was serious, so I went right to it and began planning my book. I started with my title. Peggy was very generous with her time. She helped get me back on track, and I was on my way to authorship, much to my joy and surprise.

I think it's interesting that I have never been afraid to share my life with people I didn't even know. I couldn't help but wonder why that was. Many people I know find that sharing their life is one of their greatest fears. For me, that fear dissipated because I felt I had so much to share with the world about my life and I was ready for it to unfold.

Adoption is the skeleton that holds the significant inner and outer parts of *Life Happens, Even When You are Standing Still*. The realization that stillness begins once truth arrives and you can't know what you finally find. Some of my earliest memories revolved around the concept of "the me no one saw": quietly scanning faces, searching for resemblance, for origin, for belonging.

Chapter 1

People Who Held Me

There were people who held me long before I understood I needed holding. They appeared in quiet places. They were teachers who noticed when my voice trembled, neighbors who pressed warm casseroles into my hands, friends who didn't ask why I flinched at questions about where I came from. At the time, I saw them as background characters, the kind you expect to fade before the next chapter. Only later did I realize they were the scaffolding keeping me upright. Each one softened the edges of the fear I carried, a fear that grew from not knowing who I belonged to.

I had several key people in my life. First, was my adoptive family, then later my birth family. Let me start with the dearest people I ever knew; my paternal grandparents, Charles and Clara Lapierre. Charles moved down from Canada to Chazy, New York, and settled on Lake Champlain, just across from Burlington, VT. He was a butcher by trade and had a third-grade education. My grandmother was from the Burlington area and was a housewife. She had a seventh-grade education.

Grandpa traveled across Lake Champlain and met my grandmother. They married and lived near her relatives in Burlington, VT. I'm not sure how long after they were married that they traveled by train, rented a horse and buggy, and went off to see the land in Greensboro, VT that they bought and lived on for many years. It was quite a lot of acreage. They lived on that land, selling smaller parcels over the years, until they willed the farm to my father upon their deaths.

I loved and adored my grandparents very much, especially my grandmother because we were incredibly close, and there wasn't anything I couldn't tell her. I have so many stories I could share, but I've chosen two of my favorites.

I was about 22 or 23 years old when I bought a sporty red Fiat Spider 850 convertible. I drove it home from college to show it off to my family, including my grandmother. I went to pick her up, and when we went outside, I had the top up. My grandmother had a scarf over her head, and

her words were a resounding, "Oh no. You put that top down on your car or I'm not going anywhere with you!" So, I had to put the top down, and off we went. I guess you know who the boss was!

The second story shows how much I trusted her. Around the same time, I shared that I had met a young woman I loved very much and that we planned to get married right away. I know now I was in denial about my sexual identity. My grandmother quietly and calmly said, "Well, I understand what you are talking about, but I'm wondering why you just don't live together for a while and see how it works out. Then get married if that arrangement works, but not if it doesn't." I almost fell on the floor in astonishment because I knew exactly what my parents would have said to her if they had heard that. They were very old-fashioned Christians, and in those days very few people lived together unmarried, at least that I knew of. I never married that woman or any other for many years. Somehow I had a premonition that my grandmother knew about my sexual identity and was willing to admit it before I did and stopped me from making the grievous error of getting married.

My father had two siblings; a brother, Frederick Lapierre, and a sister, Cathy Houle. My mother had three siblings; two sisters, Josephine Wells and Martha Sweatzer, and one brother, James LaMonda.

I was very saddened that I only got to meet my maternal grandparents once or twice during their lives. They lived on their old farmstead that abutted my paternal grandparents' homestead. Much later in my life, we saw them in a very dark, small apartment in New Hampshire. I can't even recall what they looked like. I would have liked to have known them better because they seemed like very nice people.

I didn't know it then, but every person who held me, guided me, prayed over me, was preparing me for the moment I would begin searching for my birth family. I thought I was merely surviving, learning how to live with the uncertainty of where I came from. But they were teaching me resilience, shaping a faith inside me that would not collapse when the truth came knocking. Their presence made the journey less frightening because I knew that even if I found answers I wasn't ready for, I had a place to return to.

I was born April 5, 1949, in St. Johnsbury Hospital in St. Johnsbury, VT at 9:25 p.m. My first name was Leo at the time of my birth, according to my original birth certificate, which I was able to obtain after a law was passed

allowing adopted children to request their original birth certificate in Vermont.

The time period between my birth and when I was brought to my adoptive parents' Arlton and Marjorie Lapierre's home was 8 months and 16 days. I was in two foster homes before I was adopted. I remained in the St.

Johnsbury Hospital until I went to live in the first of those foster homes on April 10, 1949. I arrived to live with my adoptive parents on December 21, 1949. I guess you might say that I was a Christmas present that year.

My story begins with adoption and is my foundation. The setting is New England, more specifically rural Vermont on a medium-sized dairy farm. While I wasn't born there, I grew up there. My adoptive parents provided me with all the things a baby needs; a loving home, food and shelter. With my brother, Larry's, quiet strength on one side and my sister, Rachel's, lively energy on the other, my family felt wonderfully complete.

I have very little recollection of my very early years, as I was too small to remember them. I only have two pictures from this time in my life. Purchasing a camera would have been too expensive, and getting pictures developed was out of our strict family budget. I regret not having oral histories from my parents, but a tape recorder was out of the question as it would also have been costly, and we had very little money. It would be several years before I could write down any of my information about this time of my life.

Throughout the years, it never occurred to me to pay close attention to my parents when they spoke to me so I could remember all the things they told me about what happened in those days. I wish I had written them down right away. My early memories were mostly of what my parents, relatives, and neighbors told me. The things I do remember were after-supper baths when my mom would laugh a lot as she bathed us. These were fun times for me and my siblings.

My adoptive parents' steady presence taught me what faith looks like. As we got older, my siblings and I were still small enough to all fit into one bathtub, an antique iron kitchen sink. My mother would also tell us stories about what she knew about our family during those baths. She shared stories about my parents, who grew up together because their homes were joined by a town road up over a hill. My father would ride his horse over the hill to see my mother.

Looking back now, I realize those early years were stitched together by the hands of others. The steady, imperfect, generous hands kept me afloat until I could stand on my own. I didn't yet understand the weight of what they were giving me, or how their small acts would echo through the choices I made later in life. But their care formed the first map of who I would be.

Chapter 2

Inheritance –

Traits and Patterns

I used to think inheritance was something passed down in boxes: a quilt worn thin by other hands, a photograph curling at the edges, an eye color you could trace like a map. But my lineage was a blank page for most of my life, a story unopened. The traits I carried were my stubbornness, my quiet fear, my strange faith that things happen when they are meant to seem to belong to no one. Yet even when I stood still, life kept unfolding, pulling threads together. The patterns I couldn't see were already being woven long before I found my birth family.

It arrives in whispers. Sometimes it's a familiar expression you catch in the mirror; sometimes it's a fear you can't explain. For years, I lived with the uneasy feeling that I belonged to a story I couldn't read. Adoption taught me how to build a life without a map; faith taught me how to trust that there was one anyway. When I finally began searching for my birth family, it felt less like movement and more like surrender. It was as if the patterns of my life had been patiently waiting for me to notice them.

I didn't know what I had inherited until much later. It was not the usual things, like a father's chin or a grandmother's laugh, but subtler things; a tendency to freeze when afraid, a habit of believing in what I couldn't see, a longing stitched into the seams of my days. Growing up adopted, I learned early to live in the space between what is known and what is hoped for. It wasn't until I went looking for my birth family that the patterns of my life began to reveal themselves, like constellations only visible after you turn out all the lights.

Some patterns reveal themselves only from a distance. Up close, life looks like a handful of loose threads: fear tangled with faith, longing knotted beside love. My adoption was the first stitch in a design I couldn't yet understand. For years, I stood still, afraid to pull too hard on any single strand. But inheritance has a way of calling us back to ourselves, and the day I began searching for my birth family, the design of my life shifted. The picture became clearer, the threads tightening into something whole.

I grew up thinking families were supposed to make sense. Mine didn't. It was not because it lacked love, but because half the story was missing. Adoption gave me a home, but it also gave me unanswered questions I carried like luggage I never opened. I told myself I wasn't afraid, that faith was enough. But patterns have power, and the ones running through my life finally pushed me toward the search I'd avoided for years. Finding my birth family didn't just give me answers. It showed me the inheritance I'd been living out all along.

We find the characters at this point in time on the farm, on the banks of a small, narrow, shallow brook that ran through the middle of a Northeastern Vermont farm. The trickle of cold water was loud enough to calm even three children and wash the mud from their active toes on a sunny day in the mid-1950s.

If you asked Larry, my brother, what he was doing, he would say, "Waiting for the mud pies to dam up the brook to keep the frogs back so we can swim in the pond it makes." I told you we didn't have much money, so we survived by using a healthy imagination, and these mud pies were imagined to be pancakes fried up with plenty of maple syrup. I remember that while we may have lacked money at times, we never lacked what we needed.

I also remember that I had very few originally bought clothes as I was privy to receiving my brother's hand-me-downs.

Many days were spent with the three of us kids following our father around, getting underfoot as he tried to find tasks to keep us busy and away from him. Dad was a good man. He was a hard worker and stronger for such a short man. He and Mom ran an award-winning farm. They were so proud of this, as was I, and I am still proud of these things today. They were a team, and although sometimes things got in the way, like a piece of farm equipment breaking down, nothing ever stopped them.

I remember how much I cherished being close to my Dad. I'll never forget one way he did that for me is how he held me in his lap while he drove one of the tractors he proudly owned. He let me steer it around the outside of the barn. I felt like a big shot, so manly, just like my father. I felt like I could do anything. Dad was like that: the older you got, the more responsibility you were given. To me it showed trust. Maybe more trust in me than I had in myself at the time. Writing this now, I realize he gave me many opportunities to feel manly.

As we grew older, my parents let us play unchaperoned more and more, especially outside. I remember one day after a big snowstorm. My brother and I were allowed to play in a large snow fort Dad had dug. We were playing nicely until suddenly I decided I didn't want him in my fort anymore for some forgotten reason. To get him to leave, I took my shovel and whacked him on the head and face, causing injuries that required a trip to the Emergency Room for stitches. I got spanked and a strong lecture about how unacceptable that behavior was. My parents did not spare the rod, or spoil the child, and often I was asked to pick out the stick used to spank me. People might call this corporal punishment today, but that term wasn't used then. While I hated the physical punishment, I didn't think it did me emotional harm. It was effective. As I got older, I preferred it over verbal punishment, which seemed to stay with me much longer.

It was a long time before my parents let us play unchaperoned again, but when they did, we knew not to repeat such behavior. As we grew, we incorporated new skills into larger domains of knowledge and experience and developed a greater sense of right and wrong.

We went to more parties where there was increased socialization but they were always chaperoned. I was always curious, always getting into things, asking my Dad questions about the barn and asking my Mom about adoption and other topics. It wasn't that I didn't talk to Dad. It was that he was so busy. I do remember wanting to be close to him, which often meant being in the barn under close supervision with the large cows. I was warned never to go behind or in front of the cows because they might kick. My Mom spent a lot of time in the barn, too, so we had time with her, while Dad focused on large equipment, unpredictable animals, and unexpected incidents.

My parents had a great relationship as partners running the farm. They were good role models for what a strong partnership looked like. They didn't show a lot of affection, but you could tell they were very much in love.

During the summer we were often out haying with Dad in the fields. Even before we were strong enough to lift bales, we climbed the stacks on the trailers for the spectacular views. Sometimes Dad forgot we were up there, and branches would knock us off. He had to stop the tractor, pick us up, and calm us down after the wind was knocked out of us.

I remember around age 12, Dad and I had a falling-out. I wasn't following his rules in the barn and wouldn't stop licking the cow's salt lick in the pasture. My punishment was having a cow's halter put on me and being led to the salt lick for an hour. I was always talking back to him. He later banned me from the barn for a year for being disrespectful. This only weakened our already fragile relationship. The barn was my main place of male contact; losing that hurt deeply. Rebuilding that relationship afterward was difficult because I didn't trust him to keep it going.

These were important years for building self-esteem, trust, love, self-respect, stamina, and patience. If concepts are missed during these years, they can be difficult to regain. Most importantly, I was learning to rebuild failed relationships.

During these years I also had a severe scare. One day my mother disappeared into her bedroom with no explanation and refused to come out. I was young enough to be frightened by the unknown. I felt I had lost too many people already and was too young to lose my mother. My cousins came to help take care of us. After two or three weeks, my father told us Mother was having "female problems." We had no idea what that meant. My mind filled in the blanks: Was she dead? Was she very sick? Did I cause it? This became my pattern for handling the unknown. I worried and made up explanations without validation. After four or five weeks, she came out and apologized, saying her illness had to run its course and she was okay now.

That summer, my father began building a long-awaited barn. The barn would have new stables, a milk-weight, a storage room with a bulk tank, and a new hay barn. It was modern compared to what we had before. The barn had built-in gutters that removed manure into a spreader, saving the labor of at least one man. There was a space for calves that was separate from cows. Feeding calves from bottles with big nipples could be a challenge. If the calf pulled too hard, you could be jerked off balance.

The new hay barn was four or five stories high and allowed hay to be stacked safely.

The old barn's high bays had been dangerous; hay could tumble down and smother a child. I missed the big wide window at the top of the old barn. It had such a beautiful view, but it was dangerous because you could fall out of the window. The new all-metal structure also stored machinery. Dad knew how to get the most out of everything.

Dad and I grew closer during this project. We were trusting each other again and showing unconditional love to each other for the first time in my memory. I hoped there would be many more projects together, but there weren't.

I was proud of my father. He was the smartest man I knew; not only in agriculture, but in life. I never knew the financial details of the barn and knew enough not to ask. I just knew it must have cost money, and I was proud of my parents for saving and financing it.

I took an active part in building the barn. My job was pulling bags of insulation down beams and emptying them into the eaves.

The fiberglass irritated my skin terribly. I couldn't wait to get inside and wash it off. At that time we didn't even have a shower, just a bathtub. Later, when I learned about fiberglass's negative effects, I thought about asking a doctor, but never did.

I was a neat freak and went behind the workmen cleaning up after them. This is something I still do today.

I liked the old barn because of the memories, even though it was dangerous and dark. What happened to that 100-plus-year-old barn? One night, after my brother got married, he and my sister-in-law drove into the yard. When Jane slammed her truck door, the five-story structure crumbled. Hay, timber, and equipment crashed down with a thunderous sound. Usable hay was fed to the cattle; most of the old lumber was too worn to salvage. We burned the rest. I was happy about burning the old wood. It felt like a symbolic farewell.

One new feature in the barn was a thick chain gate to prevent cows from wandering at night. Dad sometimes electrified the chain for added protection. One night, after taking the cows to pasture, he remembered he had electrified the gate but hadn't told me. He ran back, but it was too late. I had already come in contact with it. Mom and Dad wanted to take me to the Emergency Room, but I refused. I had trouble sleeping that night because of the pain. The next day was finals day at school, and I couldn't miss them. Mom checked on me at noon. The pain had eased, and the skin was healing. Nothing like that ever happened again, and Dad developed a system to alert us whenever the voltage was on. I never blamed my parents.

Around eight or nine years old, I started worrying about everything. One persistent worry was why neither of my biological parents wanted anything to do with my adoption. My mind invented explanations: Was I not good enough? Defective? Abandoned? Had they died?

Relatives sometimes visited and stayed a few days. I was always excited to see them. Families who visited often included Aunt Joe Wells, her husband Pep, and their children

Barbie, Shirley, Linda, and Howard. Martha and Johnnie Sweatzer and their children Wanda, Archie, and Paul also visited. Socializing was limited due to the demands of chores. When they visited, the women often gave each other perms to save money.

I recall one time when cousin Wanda stopped in the middle of a small brook and refused to cross. She simply didn't want to continue. This bothered me greatly, though today I can't imagine why. She could have stayed there all day. Wanting to continue my journey to see Dad, I decided to bite her. She cried and went to tell my father. It worked though because she moved! Dad told me never to bite anyone again. He said if I wanted to bite someone, to bite myself. Unfortunately, I took his advice literally and kept biting myself for years, developing a welt on my left thumb that took a year to go away. But, I never bit anyone else again.

Every morning after breakfast, Dad would drive to Greensboro to pick up my grandfather, who worked on the farm during the day and returned home at night. Gramps was a great source of conversation and humor. He smoked a pipe and cigars and kept a humidor (a special box that kept the cigars at the correct humidity level) next to his favorite chair. He was one of my favorite men because he taught me things and was kind, yet stern. I didn't know many men: perhaps three or four. I barely remember my father's brother, my uncle, because he was so much older and was always away.

Hot and humid summer days on the farm were the carefree days of our youth. My siblings and I would wake from naps and lie in the grass next to the gurgling stream, dangling our toes, watching clouds, letting our imaginations run free. We surveyed the farm buildings, green pastures, and golden hay fields. Sometimes Dad would be in the distance on his John Deere tractor and the cows would be in the meadows. In our minds, we owned it all. I felt secure, humble, and appreciative that I was chosen by this family.

Me and my siblings were the Three Musketeers. We were always together and inseparable. But as we grew older, differences emerged. My brother and sister were alike. They were blonde, blue-eyed, athletic, and outdoorsy like Dad. I was more feminine, preferred the house to the barn, and gravitated toward Mom. We grew apart in interests but maintained a good relationship.

I was always protective of my mother. Once, I saw my brother and mother fighting and ran out to stop it. Another time my mother and sister were fighting, and when I intervened, Mother told me to stay out of it. I never stepped into their conflicts again. I realized she was sticking up for them, and I was in the way.

I'm glad my Grandparents settled in Greensboro, VT. I have such good memories growing up in the country.

Chapter 3

_____

Coming of Age

Life has a way of waiting for us in the stillness, teaching us lessons we don't yet understand. Coming of age, I realize, isn't just stepping into adulthood. It's stepping into the fullness of your story, embracing both the family you were given and the one you were born into, and learning that love, in all its forms, is never truly lost.

Standing at the edge of who I was and who I am becoming, I see that life just happens. Life keeps going even when we feel frozen by fear. Adoption, faith, and reunion have taught me that the journey to yourself is never wasted, and the people who are meant to find you, eventually will.

I was twenty-something, still pretending I knew what I was doing with my life, when the notice arrived. A simple notification, nothing more, yet it cracked open a door I had spent years avoiding. Coming of age, for me, wasn't about independence or ambition. It was about facing a history I had tucked into the darkest corner of my heart. I had been adopted, yes, but I had also been afraid. Faith had carried me this far, but it was the possibility of connection, of truth, that finally made me step forward.

One fragile truth at a time.

This chapter of my life didn't start with confidence; it started with confusion. I was adopted, raised by good people, but always shadowed by the feeling that part of me lived off to the side. Coming of age, for me, meant facing that shadow instead of pretending it didn't exist. It meant owning my fear and trusting that faith would hold the pieces together. The moment I decided to search for my birth family, everything shifted. The stillness I had lived in for so long finally broke open.

I spent years trying to outrun the quiet moments when life slows just enough for the old questions to surface. Who am I? Where did I come from? What was lost before I ever learned to speak? Adoption had wrapped my beginnings in mystery, and fear kept me from unraveling the threads. But faith… faith kept tugging. My coming of age began the moment I stopped resisting and let myself listen. That was when the path toward my birth family began to reveal itself, I spent years carrying a quiet weight, a question I didn't know how to voice: Who am I, really? Adoption had painted my life with invisible lines, boundaries I didn't ask for but lived within. The fear of rejection, of never belonging, of the unknown that stretched beyond what I knew clung to me like a second skin.

Some of the most cherished memories include my father sitting me in his lap on one of his two tractors, letting me help "drive." I felt like a big shot, like a man, like *him*. As I grew, he gave me more responsibility, sometimes more than I thought I could handle. But trust builds trust. His faith in me helped me grow into myself. I used to believe that growing up was something that happened in a straight line. Childhood, adolescence, and adulthood, each their own stage clicking neatly into place. But for me, coming of age felt more like standing still in the middle of life's traffic, watching everyone else move confidently forward while I waited for a sign. Adoption taught me early how to live with questions, and faith taught me how to live with the silence between the answers. I didn't know then that was the biggest shift. The shift that would finally push me into myself was the moment I began searching for the family I had always felt but never knew.

My coming of age didn't begin with a birthday or a milestone. It began the day I admitted I was afraid—afraid of who I was, afraid of who I wasn't, and afraid of who I might find if I followed the tug to discover my own history. Adoption had given me love, but it had also given me an invisible outline of a life I wasn't born into. Faith kept whispering that the outline wasn't empty, just unfinished. When I finally started tracing it, shaky line by shaky line, I found myself walking straight toward my birth family.

Family was always close by, and in those early years, extended family often became part of the circle that helped raise us. Children are shaped not only by their parents but by the "village" of loving adults who surround them, each adding their own thread to the child's emerging story.

Imagine a warm summer day under a beautiful blue sky dotted with white, fluffy cumulus clouds. Now visualize the three of us kids riding those clouds in our imaginations, helping Dad finish his day's chores in the fields so the cows could be driven into the barn before supper. Then supper could be eaten, the cows milked, and then let out to pasture for the night. If it was a warm evening, Dad might take us to Caspian Lake Public Beach in Greensboro, VT for a refreshing swim to get us tired out before bedtime. The water sure was cold at that time of night even though it had all day to warm up. It was a lot of fun splashing each other and just swimming around doing any types of strokes that you wanted to. These were fun times with Dad and I remember them well. It also was a fun time for all of us kids to be together alone with Dad. Then the next morning, the sun would come up, the cows would be brought in, and everything would start all over again.

The day I found the family who had given me life but not a cradle, was quieter than I imagined. No dramatic scene, no lightning strike of revelation, only a slow, trembling recognition. Fear bubbled up again, the familiar shadow of doubt: Could they accept me? Could I accept them? Yet faith had taught me patience, and in that patient stillness, the pieces began to align. Adoption had made me feel fractured, invisible, and small, but the possibility of meeting them reminded me that life doesn't always happen in bursts. Sometimes it comes softly, almost imperceptibly, until one day you realize that standing still was never really standing still at all.

Every family gathering I attended as a child, I carried a hidden narrative. My smile was real, but my heart held a question that no one could answer. Who was I and where did I come from? Adoption shaped the lens through which I saw the world, a lens often tinted with fear: fear of loss, of misunderstanding, of never measuring up. Faith became my anchor, though at times it felt like clinging to a rope in a storm. And slowly, as I navigated adolescence, those threads of fear and faith intertwined. They taught me resilience and prepared me for the day I would reach beyond the safety of my known life to meet the people who were pieces of me I hadn't yet recognized.

I had always imagined life as a river, flowing whether I swam with it or sat on the shore. Adoption had given me a particular shoreline, lined with questions. Some of my questions were tender and others more jagged. Fear was the current beneath, and faith, the quiet hand that kept me from being swept away entirely. I never realized how much of my story was waiting, like sediment in the water, until the possibility of glimpsing my birth family. And then, in the meeting of the old river and new tributary, I understood: coming of age wasn't about outrunning fear or fully mastering the faith. It was about allowing life to happen, even in the spaces I thought were still.

Adolescence is often a series of small reckonings, and mine was no different. Living with adoption meant learning to navigate uncertainty, to wrestle with fear, to rely on a faith I didn't always understand but could not ignore. My birth family wouldn't erase the years of questioning or the quiet anxiety that had traveled with me, but it might reframe them. Suddenly, the story of my life felt more expansive, more complete, and more mine. I began to understand that standing still was never a failure. It was the preparation for stepping into a truth I had been seeking all along.

In our Vermont farmhouse, there was a beautiful antique Boston rocker sitting in the kitchen next to the modern refrigerator. My father sat in that chair trying to read the *Burlington Free Press* or the *Hardwick Gazette*. Then all three of us kids descended on him at once, yelling and screaming, scrambling up his pant legs and into his lap for a coveted spot as close to him as possible. My father held each of us with equal closeness. All that commotion was just to hear him tell our favorite stories about how he and his father were kids just like us. This was after a full day's work, chores, and taking Grampa back to Greensboro Village to have supper with my grandmother.

I never heard either of my parents complain. It made us feel comfortable and wanted. It was the Lapierre way, and even today it brings tears to my eyes when I summon these memories to my mind. The rocker now lives in my room, a sacred reminder of the past I carry with me.

Chapter 4

Belonging and Isolation

I used to believe that life only moved forward when I did, like when I made decisions, took risks, or stepped boldly into something new. But somewhere along my journey, I learned that life has its own rhythm, its own quiet way of unfolding, even when I am standing perfectly still. Some of the biggest shifts in my story began in moments when I felt frozen, lost between who I thought I was and who I hoped I might become.

Adoption gave me a beginning, but it also left me with a lingering question mark that followed me into adulthood. It wasn't a loud or intrusive question. It was more like a whisper that settled into the deepest part of me. Who was I before I was anyone's child? Where did the shape of my face, the tone of my voice, the tugging of my heart come from? For years, I tucked those questions away, convinced that faith alone should be enough to steady me. And in many ways, it was. Faith carried me through the storms I could name and the ones I couldn't. It kept me grounded when loneliness brushed too close and when the ache of not-knowing felt heavier than it should.

But faith doesn't erase longing. Sometimes, it gives you the courage to follow it.

My search didn't begin with a grand revelation or a sudden urge to rewrite my past. It began in an ordinary moment. One of those days when life feels a little too quiet, and your thoughts finally catch up with you. I realized that part of me was still waiting, still suspended in the space between where I came from and where I was going. Standing still had become its own kind of movement, a slow turning toward the truth I had avoided for far too long.

What if finding my identity wasn't a betrayal of the life I'd lived, but a fuller embrace of it?

Once that question took root, everything shifted. The pieces of my story that had felt scattered for so long began to point toward a path I didn't know I was ready to walk. And with every small step. I was hesitant, hopeful, and trembling when I found myself drawn closer to the people whose absence had shaped me as much as their presence someday would.

I didn't know then what discovering my birth family would ask of me, or how deeply it would rearrange the emotional furniture of my life. I only knew that I couldn't keep living with half of my story hidden in the dark. The search for identity wasn't about replacing anything. It was about uncovering the parts of myself I had never been allowed to see.

During adolescence I had many things happen to me. Early on, while I was getting older my parents were having problems with what they were going to do with me after they got me dressed to go to church and while we were all waiting for them to get ready for church. They seated me up to the piano and just let me play whatever I wanted to on it. After a while they couldn't stand the noise that came out of the piano any more. I had no idea what I was doing. My mother went under the couch cushions looking for all the loose change she could find. Then she called a lady up the road from us who taught piano lessons and asked her if she would teach me to play the piano. Luckily, she replied, "Yes." I started piano lessons soon after that day. After hours of practicing, I had the wonderful experience of accompanying my school Glee Club and playing at the installation of Grange Officers. I did this for four years. I also played for other events as well. While I felt so honored to play the piano, I also felt anxious and nervous whether I had to accompany someone or play a solo. Although I didn't keep up with practicing for years, and lost the ability to play the piano as I aged, I had many years of the wonderful calming effect at playing the piano. While the piano wasn't an instrument that you could just carry around with you, it was an instrument that could be played alone or within groups of other instruments. I found it a source of escape for me where I could take my mind to and get my thoughts and feelings out through my fingers. It's also where I felt safe and able to be by myself and be myself, where nobody could get to me. It just goes to show you what a handful of coins can get you!

 As a pianist for local Granges, I recall that I was required to play a lot of marching music during the ceremony as well as a few songs. I really liked playing marching music, so I was really in my element. I also liked being around the older adults as well as being out late during the evening. I loved that we got refreshments after the ceremony was performed.

There were seasons of my life where I felt like I was standing still while everyone else seemed to know exactly where they were going. Friends chased careers, marriages, and dreams with a confidence I couldn't imitate. I told myself I was moving forward too, but inside, something remained rooted to the ground. It was as if part of me had been left behind at the very beginning of my story. It started before I could remember and before I had any say in my life. Adoption had given me a foundation, but the foundation had cracks where unanswered questions lived. Those cracks widened in quiet moments, the moments between big life events when the world demanded nothing of me except honesty.

I learned early that you can be surrounded by people who love you and still feel unanchored. It wasn't their fault. They filled the part of my life they knew. But there was another part. It was silent, vague, shapeless and something that only I could feel. I called it my "in-between place," the space between who I was raised to be and who I might have been. It followed me into adulthood like a shadow I could neither outrun nor fully turn to face. The feeling wasn't constant, but when it showed up, it hollowed me out from the inside, leaving me both present and absent at the same time.

Faith became my map long before I ever knew what I was searching for. I didn't always follow it perfectly. Sometimes I barely followed it at all, but it was there, steady and patient. When the rest of my life felt stalled, faith was the gentle tug reminding me that stillness isn't the same as being lost. Sometimes stillness is where truth gathers itself. Sometimes it's where God prepares you for the next step, even if you feel like you're simply waiting for something unnamed.

And then, almost as if the stillness had finally broken, small clues began to appear. A name here, a document there. They were pieces of a puzzle I had carried in my heart and knapsack for years. Every step forward felt fragile, like walking across a frozen lake, unsure which parts would hold. Yet with each step, faith whispered that even uncertainty can be holy ground. I wasn't just searching for people. I was searching for myself. And without realizing it, the journey toward my birth family had already begun.

I wouldn't be honest if I didn't admit that this was one of the most difficult chapters I wrote because it was deeply personal. These years were the most uncomfortable for me. It's not a time when a light bulb goes on and it's here with no due warning of arrival. It is somewhat of a process rather than a product. Sometimes it's the product of locker room talk, or rude jokes from those you may have thought of as your friend. Sometimes there is laughter involved and or taunting. Or it may be where an adult, perhaps a parent casually mentions, "Oh this is a time when you may be approaching puberty if you haven't already, do you have any questions or something you'd like to talk about regarding it?"

For me I didn't know where or who to turn to. Once again I felt lost and alone. I just didn't think that I could talk with my parents about it because when my Mother asked me if I knew everything I wanted about sex and I said "No", she got me a book titled, *Everything You Want To Know About Sex But Were Afraid To Ask*, which was useless. In those days as far as I knew no one talked with their parents about adolescence or puberty. It was off limits. I thought that I was just a freak! I knew in my own head that others were going through it, but I just couldn't believe that I was the only one.

My bed wetting started in my early childhood and increased in frequency and amount of urine. I had so much shame and feelings of guilt and self-mutilation. I continued to not be able to go to or have any sleep-overs at my house which, in turn, made me miss out on a lot of opportunities for socialization. I feared that the word would get around school and friends' families and I would be the laughing stock of these groups of people, especially other children and adolescents. I worried that nobody would want to have anything to do with me.

It became apparent at this time in my life that I liked spending time with girls more than boys. I liked the things they talked about more. The girls did not talk about hunting and sports. I wasn't a jock or a hunter and never would be one. No matter how hard I tried.

I thought of girls with respect and never looked at them as sex objects. I think they knew this and liked me for it. I was never a threat to them. I think I was considered "safe" to be around.

I started dating during my middle adolescent years with permission from my parents. They said I could go as long as I had my older brother as a chaperone. There weren't many choices in a small, rural Vermont town, or other local neighboring towns in the area. That didn't matter to me. I guess to be honest with you, I felt a lot like Radar O'Rilley on MASH. I was very awkward!

I had a girlfriend all through Junior High and High School. The same one pretty much, except for one who I met at a National 4-H (Head, Heart, Hands and Health) Conference from Hawaii. I was not a threat over the miles. I had a girlfriend from a neighboring town here in VT my junior and senior years of High School. We got along fine and did a lot of things together including swimming in a nearby lake after her graduation. I was so thankful to her because there was no pressure on the relationship to do anything sexual. I had one girlfriend when I was at Castleton State College. I felt great, like I fit in with the other guys for the first time in my life. Again, she was not the pressuring type about sex. Sitting and talking was just fine with her. All of my girlfriends were nice, wholesome girls. I remember feeling that it was good experiencing life with different girls and girls outside my community as well.

I do remember that my male cousin took it upon himself to teach me about puberty. He started by demonstrating masturbation on himself, rather than talking about it. He took me to a remote part of his parent's barn where there was no one around. I came away with a feeling that it was dirty, and shameful. I never wanted to talk about masturbation to anyone including him and never wanted to masturbate again. He told me I could not masturbate because I wasn't old enough, only being 10 or 11. As always when someone told me, "No, you can't do that," it was just what I wanted to do, and so I did it. I guess in a sense that this was my pre-coming out as a gay person. I'm not sure there is such a thing but that's what it felt like.

One Sunday afternoon I was in my bedroom upstairs thinking that I was safe because both of my parents were downstairs. I decided that I could masturbate, because they wouldn't catch me. I must have known that there was something wrong with doing it because I knew not to get caught. I just didn't know what was wrong with it. I had also been warned by some of my male friends to be careful and not get caught by my parents because they would make a big deal out of it. I should have heard my mother coming up the stairs, but all of a sudden there she was at my door. Parents have a premonition when you are doing something you shouldn't be, or at least they think you shouldn't, and aren't afraid to use it against you. I felt that day that there was nothing wrong with masturbating, especially because so many of my male friends were doing it. I got a verbal flouncing that I was to stop and never do it again because it would make me go crazy if I didn't. Remember that I told you I was a precocious child and I responded to her by saying, "Fine, I'll only do it until I'm a little crazy!" That only made her angrier with me so then she left in a disgusted huff. But can you just imagine how her tirade about me masturbating made me feel about it? I was mortified to say the least, along with feelings of being guilt ridden and low self-esteem. This was often the way that my mother handled things she didn't want to handle for years after, even when we grew up. I remember to this day how angry I was with how she handled this whole situation and just left me to myself. I wondered if I would have handled the situation better if she had just first knocked and then talked to me about it afterward. I never knew if she ever talked with my father about it and if so, what did he say? I wondered how he would have handled it if he had been the one to find me, and maybe knocked on my door and asked me if he could come in and we talked about it? I wondered what would have happened if I had the guts to just go and knock on his door and say, "Dad I have something I need to talk about with you."

I thought that there was something terribly wrong with me when I experienced puberty, but I just didn't know what it was. I thought I was the only one this was happening to. I couldn't talk with anyone about it, especially my parents or minister. As far as I knew this just wasn't something you talked to anyone about. I was left to suffer alone with it and asked myself "Why me?" I prayed to God that he would remove this from me or make puberty only a passing phase, when in actuality it is. I thought that by having girlfriends it would throw my parents and others off track. They would think that I was normal, and then I wouldn't have to face them.

Adolescence can be difficult but even harder if you are gay and don't know it. Today it is often easier in urban areas where there are support groups that help you deal with adolescence and being gay or lesbian, but maybe not so easy in rural areas where people are often further apart. Today there are a lot more businesses and homes identified as gay friendly by flying the gay flag inside businesses and outside of homes.

While prejudice still exists against gay people and there are Hate Crimes, there's a lot more support for the LGBTQ+ Community out there than ever before.

I've never heard of Terminal Adolescence but I was sure I had it. I thought it was never going away, and it was going to do me in. When life is happening you have two choices, do something or just stand still and let it pass. I've never been much for just standing still so that is why I did things to help me with adjusting throughout my adolescence.

I always remember wanting to work because I liked money. It wasn't until later, when my parents thought that I was old enough and productive enough, that I received a weekly allowance for doing work on the farm. Work included taking care of the cattle, haying, driving the tractor, cutting and stacking wood and keeping the wood box full. I felt so proud and good about myself earning my own money. Even though there wasn't much to spend it on or places to spend it. It just felt good, and I liked saving it. I felt like I was a contributing part of the family.

I didn't like team sports, and still don't but tried solitary ones like skiing, skating, track and cross-country. I went out for basketball during high school. After much practice, I played in my first game. I got the basketball passed to me and made a basket only to find out it was for the other team and counted for them. I was unceremoniously invited to be the score keeper for my team from then on. This caused me a great deal of embarrassment, self-demoralization, and guilty feelings. This mistake made me think I couldn't do anything and get it right. It contributed a lot to my negative thoughts and feelings about myself.

I liked to join organizations with lots of people in them so I got involved with a 4-H club, a group of young folks who were into things like forestry, husbandry, and other things. I enjoyed the 4-H group and I participated in activities on a local, county, state and national level. I also enjoyed the Grange, a farmers' organization, and church with Sunday-School and Youth Group.

I wasn't particularly happy during my adolescence. I just wanted it to be over. But like it came in with no warning, no light went off to announce that it was over either. It was more like a fading away.

I tended to be shy and quiet, although I was a leader and not always a follower.

Relatives started becoming even more important to me. I liked having them around when they visited. I remember how cheerful my parents were when they were around. Cousins were of particular importance because there was increased socialization with others my own age.

There was a time during the summer of my senior year, when I was 18 years old, that I recall having a family reunion picnic at Caspian Lake Public Beach. All of the relatives had come together except for my paternal Aunt Catherine and her Husband, Uncle Ed Houle.

They hadn't shown up but their house was right next to the public beach. I decided to go over to their house and check on them. When I got there, they were just sitting there and weren't showing any signs of getting up and coming to the picnic. I asked them if they were coming and they replied with a resounding, "No". I asked them why and they told me because everyone was over at the picnic tables and talking together and no one had come over to talk with them. I extended a personal invitation for them to come over to the picnic, to which they responded by saying that they would be glad to since I was the only one who came over and extended an invitation. We walked over together to the picnic and everyone had a good time including my Aunt and Uncle. I'm glad I went out of my way, and took time away from playing with my cousins, to invite them to the picnic. It only goes to show you something I have always been good at. I would go out of my way, even if it was an inconvenience to me to make sure everyone is happy. I've always felt bad for the person who is neglected or left out or behind and I go out of my way to make them feel wanted and needed.

I particularly liked my Aunt Cathy and Uncle Ed because my Aunt Cathy was a woman before her own time, and my Uncle Ed because he was just out there. That's what I wanted to be, a man before my own time.

My Uncle Ed died when my Aunt Cathy was still a young woman. My Aunt Cathy had to find something to support herself so at her age she went at it and became the Administrator of the local Nursing Home in Greensboro, VT. I was so proud of her. She had worked very hard to open a new, more modern nursing home and close a very old nursing home that had provided services to many patients over many years to Greensboro and the surrounding communities. This nursing home is still open today and has a five star rating, which is difficult to obtain. I can't remember how long she did that for but it was quite a few years. It was quite a lot of work but she really did a great job at it. I know how much she liked it and she worked very hard to keep it going. She lived in the village of Greensboro and the nursing home was in Greensboro, so it wasn't very far from her house.

Many years later while I was in training to become the administrator of the same nursing home. I was fired because I expected people to do the job they were hired to do. The nursing director quit after not being able to handle the job. I then took on the Director of Nursing duties. As an administrator in any capacity, it has always been my philosophy that for the most part you can expect people to do the job they were hired to do or work with them to understand what they are expected to do and give them time to change to do it or you have the right to fire them.

One thing that I didn't agree with Aunt Cathy about was that she wouldn't hire any male staff to take care of female patients. I really wanted to provide patient care to all patients. This was a subject that we never broached so I never got a chance to express my feelings. I do have to say that this way of thinking was very usual for that day and age. I think it was one reason that I accepted it and didn't say anything about it. But I always really regretted it.

She was a clever woman. She knitted and crocheted the most wonderful clothing such as mittens and sweaters. She smoked like a chimney. At that time, it wasn't unusual for women to smoke. She bought the most outstanding yellow Volkswagen (VW) Beetle. She drove it without reserve all over the place. There wasn't another one like it in the town of Greensboro or any other neighboring town for miles around. Now you see many around town!

One situation was mixed when it came to relatives. I had one maternal uncle, my Mother's brother, who I loved dearly. His name was Uncle Bud. I remember that when he was sober, he was one of the best people I knew. He was so kind and loving. However, when he was drunk he was one of the worst men you would ever want to know. During these times, he was slobbering, crying, falling down drunk and slurring his speech. I was always afraid of him when he was in that condition. I remember that we would get a call and then my father would always have to go to a nearby town and get him stumbling out of a bar, bring him home, and sober him up until the next time. Sobering him up meant lots of coffee, showers and changing of clothes because he would vomit on himself. It certainly wasn't a pretty picture. Then he would be taken by my folks to a group of people who help others to get sober and stay sober. But the incidence of him staying sober was rare to nothing.

I recall the New Year's Eve of my senior year when he was working in one of the lodges up on Mount Mansfield of Stowe, VT. While there, he committed suicide by drinking large amounts of sterno, which is the liquid that was lit on fire and placed under chafing dishes to keep the food in them hot. His body wasn't found for three or four days afterwards, therefore there could be no open casket at his memorial service. No one seemed to know that Uncle Bud was particularly depressed and no suicide note was left. Many questions went unanswered as to why he had done this. I was close to him and we talked a lot, but I'm not sure I would have recognized depressive symptoms strong enough to leading to committing suicide. I was devastated and didn't know what I was going to do. I remember becoming depressed and remaining depressed for days after getting the news. His death was such a loss and I was at such a loss as to what to do to get over it. I just didn't know what I was going to do to get over it. In fact I thought I would never get over it, and sometimes have trouble with it when I think about it today. It had a major impact on how I thought and felt about death and suicide, and how I dealt with it for a long time after. I also remember that my Mother was particularly kind and gentle toward me during that time, and kept checking in with me all the time. I was eternally grateful at that time and even today for the kindness that my mother extended to me during that time. It made it all bearable at a time that I really needed it.

I think one of the reasons I had so much trouble with it was that I was trying to deal with my own uncertain thoughts and feelings about suicide also at the time. I just couldn't merge the thoughts and feelings about suicide with the reality, which this opportunity provided to me. I know I was terribly uncomfortable with it.

While there was a lot of depression, turmoil and we were always considered poor up through these years and during my adolescent years, one thing I constantly kept in mind was that we were rich in many other ways that may not have been tangible and outright visible, such as love, for each other and as a family. I think you know which one I would rather have, even to this day.

In the end, my search for identity was never a straight path but a series of pauses, questions, and quiet prayers whispered into the unknown. I spent years believing that stillness meant stuckness, that being adopted meant living with an unfillable space inside me. But life kept moving even when I couldn't, nudging me toward trust, toward faith, toward the courage to keep hoping. *Life Happens — Even When You Are Standing Still* is not just a title; it could become my truth the moment I found the people who shared my blood. In their faces, in their stories, could I discover that the lost child I carried within me? I had been waiting not for movement, but for belonging.

Chapter 5

Legacy or Unproductive

In the quiet spaces of my life like the ones where I felt suspended between who I was and who I hoped to become, I often wondered what kind of legacy a person could leave when they felt unproductive, unseen, or unfinished. This chapter marks the place where the world kept moving while I felt lost in my own story, adopted into love yet searching for the truth that formed me. I didn't know then that faith was already doing the quiet work of stitching together the family I had and the one I had yet to find.

In my early adulthood, I spent a lot of energy and anxiety beginning my educational journey, starting with my acceptance into Castleton State College (CSC) in 1973. The school later became Castleton University and eventually Vermont State University, Castleton. I never completed a degree there, but I enjoyed it immensely and it served as a diving board into higher education.

Later on, while working at St. Elizabeth's Hospital and studying for my master's degree, I met Peter. He became my partner for more than eleven years. I met him at the Pines on Fire Island. We shared a beautiful co-op (where people buy shares in the corporation that owns the building. The community supports one another in many ways) in New York City and a wonderful house on Fire Island, a gay mecca about twenty-five or thirty miles outside the city.

Peter and I met during a tea dance at the Pines and made plans to meet again at the regular disco later that evening. Tea dance was a toned-down version of disco. It was music ramping up while men danced in their bathing suits, coming straight (no pun intended) from the beach, often not shaved or showered. The Tea dance began around four or five in the afternoon and ended around six or seven. Then everyone went home, took a nap, showered, had dinner, and later headed back to the dance area where disco blasted until one, sometimes three, in the morning.

There were no cars on the island except for emergency vehicles. Our house was in one of the largest communities there, simply called the Pines. Because there were no cars, there were no real roads. Instead, we pulled a little Red Flyer wagon along the boardwalk, up to our house. The boardwalk was our main thoroughfare, with smaller walkways leading to people's homes. Everyone pulled groceries, liquor, luggage, basically whatever was needed, in those little red wagons. In a way, it felt like returning to childhood.

The only way to reach the island was by ferry. I loved that ferry ride. As the water widened between the mainland and the island, I felt the tension leave my body. The tension wouldn't return until we made the trip back on Sunday afternoons. It was as if each muscle relaxed, stiffness floating away, freeing me to breathe deeply again.This life was so different from the constant pressure of life in the city.

Fire Island, especially the Pines, felt like stepping into another life. The island sat out in the ocean, but it was filled with people who lived unencumbered by New York City's demands. Not far from our house was a home that held the piano on which *Hello Dolly!* was composed. People there seemed freer, lighter. The Atlantic Ocean was only a ten or fifteen-minute walk from our doorstep. I loved being so close to it. I loved swimming nude whenever the tides allowed, feeling the saltwater carry away everything heavy.

Cherry Grove, a few miles' walk from the Pines, was more of a gay and lesbian community at the time. It wasn't as glitzy as the Pines, but it was warm and welcoming. I remember walking from the Pines to the Grove on nights when the moon was full. The stars spread across the ocean like glitter, the moonlight turning the water into a path you wished you could walk on.

On Sundays, when it was time to return to the mainland, we'd take a chartered bus from the ferry landing back into New York City. Those rides were full of laughter, conversation, and the soft ache of saying goodbye. We often had plans already made for the week ahead.

For years, I believed that legacy was something other people inherited. It was something written in bloodlines and family stories told at holiday tables I never sat around. My own story felt like a half-finished sentence. I told myself it didn't matter, that faith should be enough to settle the restless ache. But in quiet moments, the question always returned like a stubborn tide: What am I built from, and what am I meant to build? It was hard not to wonder if my life was drifting, if my days were something to endure rather than shape.

There were times when I confused stillness with failure. When life didn't move fast enough, I blamed myself for standing still and for not knowing where to go or what to claim as my own. Adoption can leave a strange silence. It is an emptiness where history should live. In that silence, it's easy to believe you're unproductive, that your roots never took hold, so your branches can't possibly bear fruit. But even then, faith whispered that standing still wasn't the same as being lost. Sometimes stillness is just a breath held before a deeper truth reveals itself.

I often wondered what legacy meant for someone who didn't know the people they came from. Was my path determined before I ever arrived, or was I free to write it myself? The world speaks loudly about productivity. It is measured in achievements, milestones, and tidy progress. But adoption taught me that beginnings are not always straightforward, and faith taught me that they don't have to be. I learned that I wasn't an accident in anyone's story; not my birth family's, not my adoptive family's, and not God's.

What I didn't know then was that life was quietly preparing me. The restlessness, the drifting, the unanswered questions weren't signs of being unproductive but signs of growth. Every desperate prayer, every moment suspended between who I was and who I might become, was part of a journey I couldn't yet see. Standing still didn't mean stagnation; it meant I was being held until the time was right.

These were the best years of my life. I had a great job. I lived in a city I loved. I had a warm and supportive family, and I was with the man I loved. Nothing could have been better.

What I learned, slowly and sometimes reluctantly, was that life keeps unfolding even when you feel rooted to the same spot. In my early adulthood, whole seasons changed around me while I was still trying to decide what direction to walk in. Relationships, I discovered, weren't effortless. They asked for attention, honesty, and a willingness to let someone see the parts of me I wasn't sure about. When I finally allowed myself to open the door a little wider, to listen more than I talked, to notice the world beyond my own worries, everything felt fuller. The missteps still came, but I began to understand that moving through them taught me as much as the sweet moments did.

I also learned that waiting wasn't enough. Life nudged me to work for the things I hoped for. Some semesters I pushed too hard, took on more than I could manage, and paid for it in exhaustion and slipping grades. Adjusting wasn't failure; it was part of finding out who I was and how I functioned. Love, too, asked for effort. Love did not ask for the kind of effort that drains, but the kind that deepens. When I let myself feel it instead of analyzing it from a distance, it gave back more than I expected. Little by little, those lessons carried me forward, shaping a life I was finally willing to step into.

Some drifts are quiet. They are so quiet you only recognize them in hindsight, like noticing how the light changes between seasons. My life was shaped by such subtle currents. As an adoptee, I learned early how to float between identity and imagination, belonging and wondering. But somewhere along the way, I lost track of where I was heading.

During my middle adulthood, life began to settle down. I call these my "education years," because I earned three degrees in Nursing within fifteen years. At age 35, in 1975, I completed my Bachelor of Science in Nursing (BSN) from Trenton State College (now The College of New Jersey). In 1980, at age 40, I earned a Master of Arts in Psychiatric Nursing at Rutgers University. In 1985, at age 45, I completed a PhD in Adult Psychiatric Nursing at the University of Alabama at Birmingham (UAB).

With each degree, my opportunities grew. I began receiving job offers with more prestigious titles and larger salaries. My mission felt complete.

But there was one problem: the day after I received my PhD diploma was, unexpectedly, one of the worst days of my life. I had achieved something I never imagined possible. A boy raised on a dairy farm in Vermont, starting out in a one-room schoolhouse, now holding three advanced degrees. I hadn't even dared to dream of this. So what was I supposed to do now? For the first time, I felt like there was nothing left for me to reach for. Or so I thought.

I didn't begin writing this book until I was 76 years old, and sometimes I wonder if I waited too long. Back then, the day after graduation, I felt like my life had suddenly lost its purpose. I had prepared for the work but not the ending. Those feelings blindsided me, coming out of nowhere and hitting me between the eyes.

I used to believe that standing still meant holding my place, but life shifts beneath your feet even when you don't move. Growing up adopted, I learned a practiced kind of gratitude. It was one that keeps you polite and agreeable even when your heart whispers questions you're afraid to speak out loud. Over the years, that whisper became a low tide pulling at me. It was subtle, persistent, familiar in a way I couldn't name. I didn't know the drift had already begun, nudging me away from the version of myself I worked so hard to maintain.

There were days when I felt suspended between two worlds. One I knew and one I sensed but couldn't see. The feeling wasn't dramatic; it was more like waking up in a room that looks almost, but not quite, like your own. My family loved me, and faith kept me steady, but something inside me remained unanchored. I carried a quiet ache. It was not an emptiness of loss, but an emptiness of mystery. I prayed for peace, not realizing I was praying for a path. The lostness wasn't a flaw; it was a map pointing toward something or someone I had yet to find.

After completing my degrees, I felt proud. I had struck out on my own, making things work despite humble beginnings and limited means. No one else in my family had done what I had done. Despite all that pride, I made the mistake of withdrawing into myself. I kept wondering: *What do I do now? Who am I without school?* Education had been the rhythm of my life for so long that I couldn't imagine life without it.

Sitting alone in my apartment that first day, I refused to feel sorry for myself. I talked to myself, like I often do, and decided to take action. I made plans, called friends, went out to dinner, and got a good night's sleep. The next morning, I returned to my job at UAB, something I was fortunate to have.

Being around people I liked and respected helped. I also knew I would be moving to Washington, D.C. in a year, a place I had long wanted to be.

Eventually, I ended up moving back to Vermont to live with my sister, Rachel, but just when things seemed promising another challenge arose. Shortly after the move it became apparent that she was going through a difficult time and not managing her substance abuse well. One thing I brought back to Vermont with me was that I had worked hard to get and remain sober for a number of years. I was concerned when I realized that I hadn't seen my sister in a few weeks. Fear of the unknown had contributed to my addiction and I was determined not to let that happen again. I knocked on her door expressing my concern and asking for a face to face. When she finally opened the door, I was shocked to see the condition of her room with beer bottles scattered around. At that moment, I realized I needed to prioritize my own sobriety and living with her was jeopardising it. I felt guilty, even ashamed, for wanting to leave. Soon after, to protect myself and be closer to my established church and new friends, I purchased a condo in Morrisville and moved there. The congregation, choir, and pastor provided a stabilizing and supportive environment that I desperately needed. Although I felt like I was abandoning my sister, I knew I needed to go. I missed the companionship of living with her, but thankfully we remained close.

Soon after moving, I met a young teenage boy named Justin and his adoptive mother, Kristin, through the church. I liked them immediately. I felt needed by them. Someone needing me was a magnet for me, and also a warning sign. Being needed has always pulled me in quickly, and at that time, loneliness made me vulnerable. We began spending time together. We enjoyed meals, movies, bowling, and talking together. A year and a half later, Kristin and I married. We both believed that companionship and shared responsibility would create stability, especially for Justin.

But Justin struggled with impulsive behaviors. This included running away and often getting into legal trouble. His behaviors strained all of us. He manipulated situations to get electronics or attention, creating tension between Kristin and me. The arguments between all of us increased. We hoped a fresh start might help, so we planned a move to a better school district near Waterbury, VT. I withdrew all my retirement savings to buy the house in cash.

Just an hour before I was set to move in, Justin called and told me not to come. He and Kristin had decided the move wasn't a good idea because of all the arguments. I was furious. I felt hurt, used, and powerless.

I filed for divorce and vowed never to speak to them again. It felt childish, perhaps, but it was the only way I could protect myself at the time.

For a year I lived alone with few furnishings. Then, out of nowhere, Justin called inviting me to lunch with him and Kristin. They acted as if nothing had happened and presented a plan for them to move into the house I had bought. Against my better judgment and driven by loneliness, I agreed. I didn't tell anyone, not even my close friend and niece,

Tracy, because I didn't want to hear the truth. History might repeat itself.

And it did.

For a year things seemed better. Then the yelling returned. Justin retreated into his room, speaking only when necessary, especially when he wanted something. The tension grew unbearable.

Then I fell down a flight of stairs and broke my left shoulder. This added pressure on Kristin, who was already overwhelmed. The relationship deteriorated quickly. I became so distraught I wanted to end my life. One evening, Kristin and Justin took me to the emergency room out of concern. I told the doctor honestly what was happening and that I needed hospitalization to stay safe.

I spent two of the best weeks of my life in the psychiatric unit at the hospital in Berlin, VT. When I was discharged, I moved in with two loving church members, David and Judy Bickford, until I could get back on my feet. They taught me many things, but most importantly, they showed me the true meaning of a loving relationship.

Eventually, I filed for divorce again. This time I knew it was the end of our relationship. I married Kristin and divorced her twice. I hope that experience taught me something lasting about relationships and self-protection.

I experienced unexpected emotional reactions, even after great achievements like receiving my PhD. Relationships don't always last, no matter how much hope one brings into them. By the time I recognized the distance between where I started and where I stood, the journey had already remade me. Adoption shaped my beginning, the feeling of being lost shaped my middle, and faith carried me through the quiet uncertainties.

Chapter 6

_____

Looking Back,

Looking In

Looking back is like turning to studying an old photograph.

A picture where I recognize the face, but not the story behind the eyes. For so long I lived suspended between two identities: the child who was chosen and the adult who still wondered why he had been given away. Maybe there is a place where the two might meet.

Vermont had become the first U.S. state to create a civil union status for same-sex couples. While civil unions offered many state-level benefits like legal inheritance, hospital visitation, spousal support, and more, they were still denied the name "marriage." This carried no federal recognition, since federal law at the time did not recognize same-sex marriages, and it was unclear whether civil unions would be honored across state lines. Vermont chose a cautious but pioneering step: equal protections without the name.

Vermont has its own story of realization. Though rural and small, it has long embraced independence and progressive thought. It played a pivotal role in the history of marriage equality in the United States. Sexual-orientation protections were passed as early as 1992, and many Vermonters took pride in fairness.

On December 20, 1999, the Vermont Supreme Court issued a landmark ruling in Baker v. Vermont, brought by three same-sex couples who had been denied marriage licenses. In response, the legislature created civil unions, effective July 1, 2000, granting same-sex couples nearly all state-level rights of marriage. Vermont became the first state to establish such a legal status.

Nearly a decade later, in 2009, the push for full marriage equality returned. The legislature passed Bill 5.115, and though Governor Jim Douglas vetoed it, the legislature overrode the veto the next day. On September 1, 2009, same-sex couples began marrying in Vermont. This time not because the courts required it, but because lawmakers believed it was right. Protections for religious institutions were included, respecting both equality and conscience.

After marriage equality became law, existing civil unions remained recognized, though no new ones were issued. A historic marker now stands at the Vermont State House honoring the court ruling and civil union law. Vermont's quiet leadership offered a model for the nation, proving change can be both courageous and measured.

As I write on Thursday, September 11, 2025, the anniversary of that fateful day, I find myself thinking about all the goodbyes I never got to say. I never had the chance to say goodbye to my adopted brother, because my sister-in-law didn't tell me he was dying until it was too late. I never got to say goodbye to my adopted sister, because she died suddenly and unexpectedly. I began to wonder how many people alive today never got to say goodbye to their loved ones on that day in history when America was attacked in New York City. Without those goodbyes, a piece of my life always felt missing.

Looking back now, I can see how much of my childhood I spent trying to read the room. I was searching for hints, clues, anything that might explain the ache that lived in my ribcage. I didn't have a name for it then. I only knew that sometimes, even while surrounded by people who loved me, I felt like a puzzle piece placed in the wrong box close to fitting, but never quite snapping into place.

Living with that kind of quiet uncertainty shapes you. It sharpens your hearing for the smallest details: a tone of voice, a half-told story, the way someone sidesteps a question. For me, faith became the one place where I didn't feel out of step. It asked nothing of my history and everything of my heart. Maybe that's why I clung to it, it was the first place that didn't require explanations in order for me to feel at home.

But even faith has a way of circling you back to the questions you try to bury. Mine kept whispering: *If you believe God created you with purpose, aren't you curious where you came from?* I resisted that whisper for years. I told myself it didn't matter, that the family who raised me was enough. Yet deep inside, the lost part of me kept tapping its foot, waiting for me to stop running from the truth.

I felt that if I finally found my birth family, it would feel like stepping into a room I had dreamed about but never dared to enter. The familiarity might hit first. The eyes, the gestures, the laughter that felt like it had been waiting for me. The feeling of being lost that had followed me for so long might not disappear, but it might loosen its grip. I realized I wasn't looking back anymore. I would be looking in and for the first time, the reflection might look like mine.

As I grew older, life grew easier in some ways and harder in others. I never wanted to retire. I pictured myself being found at my job someday with my head resting on my folded arms. I would be gone, not sleeping. I never imagined myself aging. I loved working and never wanted to stop. I couldn't imagine a life of simply sitting still.

Work was a big part of me and still is today, which is why I wrote this book. I used to say I would have to die to stop working. Of course, that turned out not to be true.

I worked until I was about 66 years old. I started out on the farm, doing whatever chores were needed: caring for cattle, baling hay, and countless other tasks. My first paid job outside the family was at Greensboro High School, assisting the janitor after classes, before heading home to help my father with evening chores.

I worked summers at a local lodge as an assistant to the chef until it closed each winter. I worked during college breaks on the farm. I also worked at the snack bars on Mount Mansfield in Stowe, VT. I was never afraid of work. The only time I did not work was when I was attending college.

I always had one job I could count on: keeping my mother's wood box full. She cooked on an old iron stove that had belonged to my paternal grandmother. I chopped and stacked the wood, filled the box, and kept the fire going. This was important especially on cold winter days, since the stove provided both meals and heat.

Looking back now, I see that every moment I thought I was standing still was actually pulling me forward. Adoption left me with questions too heavy for a child to articulate, and feeling lost became a kind of second skin. But faith nudged me inward, reminding me that my story wasn't scattered. It was simply waiting.

Finding my birth family might not answer everything but it might offer a place for my heart to rest. It could finally recognize itself after years of wandering.

Chapter 7

I Never Wanted

to Hold a Weapon

From a very young age around ten or eleven years old, I made a firm vow that I would never go into the military. I knew that if I couldn't kill animals, there was no way in the world I could kill a person. I never imagined that later in life I'd eat those words. I discovered I could help *save* lives in the military as a nurse.

When I was about sixteen or seventeen, my father took me into the woods and made me shoot a rifle just to prove I could. I hit the target, which was an old tin can. He was satisfied, and so was I. It didn't change my feelings about killing. If I didn't have to kill anything, that was fine by me. I never went hunting with my father, my brother, or anyone else. I never will.

After dropping out of Castleton State College, I received a letter from the United States Military stating that I had to report to New Hampshire for an overnight stay and an induction physical the next day. The Vietnam War draft was active at the time. The news terrified me. I was strongly against the war and against joining any branch of the military.

My anxiety spiraled. My pulse went over two hundred, and because of that, the nurses who were evaluating me kept me overnight. The next morning, it was still around two hundred. I persuaded them to let me return home to be evaluated by my own doctor. When he took my pulse, it was back to normal, eighty-four. This was what I expected and then I told the military personnel performing my physical that my anxiety was elevating my pulse.

I also knew my medical history included treatment for depression, and if that information was still in my record, it could keep me out of the service. It was there. I was classified as 4F, which meant Not Fit for Military Service. I thought I should have felt relieved, but instead I had mixed feelings, including the familiar sting of rejection.

I received a letter dated December 8, 1969 stating that a Form 52 was enclosed, declaring me "not acceptable for induction under current standards." It also said I would be re-examined in six months. That never happened.

It wasn't until fourteen or fifteen years later that the military re-entered my life. I was working at the Veterans Administration Medical Center in New York City and needed more money. Needing money was a theme throughout my life. At the time, the VA had a policy that if you worked for them, you also had to work part-time for the military.

So I mailed a card with my contact information to a National Guard recruiter and arranged a meeting. I remember the cold, blustery fall day as I walked to his office at the lower tip of Manhattan. He explained the job, the benefits, the nurse's role in the National Guard, one weekend a month and two weeks of annual training.

I asked if he knew about my 4F status. He said, "Yes. But look what you've accomplished with your education and career. We would be proud to have you in our service. You are well qualified." Those words made me feel incredibly good. Then he added, "Just keep your mouth shut. Nobody needs to know about your status except you and me." He told me he could get me the rank of Captain, maybe even Major. I never made Major and I stayed a Captain throughout my time with the military.

Truth be told, I didn't know anything about rank. I just nodded along. Later, when I told my friends, they exclaimed, "Take it! All that with no officers' training? Are you kidding?"

I was in the process of moving to Florida, so I waited until I got there to be sworn into the Florida National Guard (FLNG). Once I joined, I was surprised by how much I enjoyed it. At my first drill, I initiated closing the helicopter doors when transporting patients. This was something important for safety, especially with patients who might behave unpredictably even while restrained. I felt useful. My contributions were recognized. My self-esteem, self-respect, and self-worth rose. I looked forward to drills every month.

Despite being a lifelong nonconformist, I loved the structure and clarity of the Guard. I didn't expect that. But I think it was the transparency. There were no unnecessary questions, no complications. Just do your job.

I was also excited about the uniform. I felt that something about the uniform felt like joining a new chapter of life. I enjoyed serving my country. As a nurse in an EVAC Hospital, I could combine mental and physical health care, something I rarely got to do in my civilian job. I remember one soldier in particular who had suffered burns to 98% of his body in a tank fire. I learned to debride dead skin so that new, healthy skin could grow. The work was intense but deeply meaningful.

About a year later, I moved to Birmingham, Alabama to begin my PhD at the University of Alabama at Birmingham. I joined a new EVAC unit. It was the same type of work but with different people. Again, I found community and support.

Annual training in Alabama was different. One summer, we were taken to a swampy location where equipment for the EVAC Hospital was dropped by helicopter at 1:00 AM. We were required to fully assemble it by 8:00 AM. I was terrified as there were alligators and poisonous snakes in the area, and I'm deathly afraid of both. But I did it. I was very proud of myself.

I served as head nurse of a Step-Down Unit for simulated medical-surgical cases. One morning, I suddenly noticed a soldier standing beside me with a loaded rifle. Behind him was a large helicopter and my tent. He told me he and another soldier were guarding a Three-Star General who had come to inspect the EVAC Hospital. I was told not to speak to the General unless he asked me a question.

He stayed for a little over an hour. Later, my Chief Nurse hurried to my tent, breathless, and asked what I had said to him. I told her I simply explained what we did and showed him around. She said the General told her that in his thirty years in the Army, no one had ever given him such a clear explanation of a Step-Down Unit. She praised me for it.

At another annual training, I was assigned to lead a team of fifteen to twenty soldiers preparing equipment for those deploying to Desert Storm. I created a checklist, set up an assembly line, and ensured that every necessary item went into each duffle bag. We reached 100% compliance. I treated the enlisted soldiers well. I took them out for ice cream on a hot day and they worked their hearts out. I received an Army Achievement Medal/Ribbon for my leadership on that project.

On another training, right before we were to leave for the Panama Canal Zone, a young couple in the unit decided to get married. They skipped a honeymoon because of deployment. I felt empathy for them and gave them the key to my hotel room so they could spend one night together. I knew I could get in trouble for that, but I took the risk anyway. That was always my way. I would take the side road to help someone else.

About a year after graduating from the University of Alabama (UAB), I moved to Washington, D.C. for a job I had always dreamed of. I became Head of Nursing Education on the St. Elizabeth's Campus with the National Institute of Mental Health Neuropsychiatric Research Hospital. The diversity of staff from across the U.S. and around the world made it feel like I was working at the United Nations.

I helped develop a tool that measured changes in patients receiving new medications. I co-authored an article and presented it at a conference. There were thirty-six patients from around the world across the three units.

I was nominated by my Chief Nurse to advise the Surgeon General of the United States on Mental Health for families nationwide. It was one of the greatest honors of my career. Combined with beginning my private practice, I felt like I had reached a professional peak.

After ten years, however, two social worker officers began harassing me. They were accusing me of seeing private patients during duty hours. I could prove otherwise, but the constant stress wore me down. Eventually, I resigned my commission with the U.S. Public Health Service and entered the private mental health sector.

I never wanted to hold a weapon, yet for so many years I carried invisible ones. They were the fear, doubt, and defenses I built to survive what I didn't understand about myself. Life kept placing unexpected things in my hands: a rifle, a uniform, a military career I never imagined, and eventually the truth of my own story. Each one taught me something I didn't know I needed to learn. If anything, my journey showed me that the things we swear we'll never do sometimes end up leading us to the parts of ourselves we'd been missing all along. Staying open, even reluctantly, allowed me to grow into a fuller version of who I was meant to become.

Chapter 8

A Sudden Realization

A sudden realization unfolded in my life the way dawn does. It shows up softly at first, then all at once. For years, my journey through adoption and identity felt like wandering in circles, proving again and again that life happens even when you stand still. Even when I felt lost, faith whispered that something greater was shaping my steps. I couldn't have imagined how right that whisper was.

When the truth of my birth family might finally appear, I was already carrying years of confusion about who I was, especially around my sexuality. Coming out today is often friendlier, easier, and supported by more resources, but at the time I had no such guidance. I worried that I had somehow done something wrong, even wondered if I could "go back" to being straight. At my lowest points, I feared my feelings were an incurable illness. Some nights I cried myself to sleep, wondering if the only escape from the turmoil in my mind was self-destruction. But even then, something in me held on.

It was a vulnerable time, and I wish I'd had someone trustworthy to guide me through it. There is meaningful support on all levels, including physical, emotional, and spiritual for those navigating coming out. Being gay isn't something you catch or something that can be cured; it's simply one way of being human. It can bring joy and confusion, clarity and fear, but it is never something to be ashamed of.

As time went on, my refusal to deal with coming out only deepened my misery. Then one day, while working at a firm that manufactured rifles, a man my age invited me to dinner. It happened to be my birthday, and I had no other plans. After dinner he showed me pictures. First , he showed me pictures of nude women. These didn't interest me. Then he showed me pictures of nude men. I was very interested in those pictures. He asked if I was gay. I was uncertain so I told him I didn't know. He asked if I'd ever been to a gay bar. I hadn't. When he offered to take me to one, I said yes.

Walking into that bar felt like arriving someplace my life had been quietly leading me toward. For a moment, I thought I had died and gone to heaven. He stayed a while and then left me on my own. I had no trouble meeting other men. As I prepared to leave, a bouncer warned me that a fight was about to break out between several men vying for my attention. She told me not to return before the following Saturday and to dress down when I did. That strange introduction became my doorway into coming out.

I returned every Saturday. I met people, made friends, and slowly accepted myself. My depression lifted, and so did my self-esteem. For the first time, I could look at myself and feel at peace.

Things have changed dramatically since then. Coming out is far easier today, even in rural areas where silence or shame once ruled. People now understand that depression and confusion around coming out require compassion, not condemnation. Finding a guide, someone trustworthy and steady can make the journey safer and clearer. Self-acceptance alone is an enormous step.

My fifth and final lover should never have happened. I was an easy target. I was lonely, out of practice, and on vacation when I met Leo in a gay bar in Ogunquit, Maine. By then the pattern was familiar. Relationships began with fireworks and ended in smoke. I wasn't willing to let anything unfold slowly. Denial came easy, and so did ignoring the lessons of my past.

My life has never moved in a straight line. Often I felt motionless while everything around me rushed forward including careers, families, and answers I couldn't find. Stillness doesn't always mean being stuck. Sometimes it's the only place quiet enough for truth to surface. It was in that stillness that I first admitted how deeply I needed to know my beginnings, and once spoken, that desire could no longer be ignored. Life happens even in the pauses and sometimes the pauses let us finally hear ourselves.

In that moment of sudden realization, the scattered pieces of my story finally aligned. I wasn't just an adoptee searching for a name or a face. I was someone carried by a faith that refused to let me drift too far from myself. Trying to find my birth family wouldn't erase the years of feeling lost, but it could soften them and give them shape. For the first time, I felt the ground steady beneath me. Life had been moving all along. I had only just caught up.

Chapter 9

The Shape of Knowing

There were times I felt completely adrift, as if I were moving through life without a map or compass. Not knowing where I belonged or even who I truly was made the days blur together. Yet looking back, I see that those moments were part of the shape forming beneath the surface. The uncertainty, the longing, the quiet questions weren't just obstacles. They were lines in the sketch, guiding me toward a fuller understanding of myself and, eventually, the possibility of being guided toward the family I had been separated from at birth.

I began my education in a one-room schoolhouse tucked inside a larger building. I can't remember how many children were there, only that there weren't many. It felt almost like a private school because we received so much attention, even though only one teacher handled each class. When

I entered Junior High, another local school merged with ours, doubling the number of students. The playground had few toys, so recess was held on the front lawn under the watchful eye of our teacher, who was married to the Principal. No one wanted to get sent to the Principal's office; you'd receive the combined wrath of both the teacher and the principal.

Despite occasional teasing about being adopted, I liked school and felt relatively safe. My only real worry was whether I'd be allowed to use the bathroom in time. I always feared the embarrassment of wetting my pants. This was something that, thankfully, rarely happened. I advanced through the grades without being held back. Even then, I found myself quietly interested in boys. I assumed it was a phase everyone went through. There was more homework in Junior High, which I enjoyed because it gave me an excuse to avoid barn chores. After school I had to change into barn clothes and help before supper. Puberty arrived awkwardly but quietly, and the school eventually moved out of the one-room building into a larger, more modern one, up on a hill.

High School brought new freedom. I loved switching classrooms for different subjects. It helped me feel mature. I took mostly college-prep courses with a few business classes like typing, and I'm glad I did. Even today, I believe in learning something new every day, right up to the day I die.

I stayed busy with being Co-Salutatorian, yearbook editor, class officer, piano student, and accompanist for the Glee Club. Belonging to these activities boosted my self-esteem. School gave me structure and purpose, and even my incontinence improved for a time.

The summer before college, I worked on my parents' farm and at Lake View Inn. I always wanted a college education. My father had a degree in Agriculture after he had switched from Engineering. At least one person in the family had done what I hoped to accomplish.

The shape of knowing is not a straight line; it's like a widening circle. I once believed stillness meant stagnation. I felt if I wasn't moving, I was falling behind everyone who seemed to know where they belonged. But life kept happening to me, around me, and through me, even when I stood perfectly still. Adoption taught me early that beginnings often come in pairs: the story you're given, and the story you must grow into. Much later I realized that faith fills the space between those two stories.

I was thrilled and terrified when I left for college. The family joke was that I drove off so fast you couldn't see my car through the smoke from the exhaust. The truth is my parents dropped me off, and saying goodbye was emotional. Orientation was exciting for me. I made friends quickly and loved the classes. Living in a dorm, eating in a cafeteria, and being surrounded by so many people was new to me. Even with all the noise, I often felt lonely. This was something that became a recurring theme in my life.

Castleton University in Vermont was small but lively. It was close enough to the New York border that many of us piled into cars

on Thursday evenings for drink specials.
Friday classes were rough. There were lots
of hung-over students. I met people from
urban backgrounds and cultures that were
very different from my rural upbringing.
Even though I carried worry like a second
skin, I made it through my first semester
with good grades.

I also had to accept certain shortcomings
that were both physical and emotional. I was
small and still shopping in the boys'
department, much to my embarrassment. I
was often teased by the bigger guys in my
friend group, yet I kept going.

By my sophomore year I had more freedom
in choosing classes and enjoyed college
even more. I worked the same summer jobs
as before, and when I returned to campus, I
arrived in my proudest possession. It was a
VW Beetle I bought with help from my
parents. The same type of car that Aunt
Cathy had.

Before spring semester, I met with both the
Dean of Nursing and the Dean of Education
and received approval to pursue an

Associate Degree in Nursing alongside a Bachelor's in Education. It meant long days with clinical sessions starting at 7 A.M. and classes that ran until 9 P.M. but I didn't mind. My plan was to finish nursing first, pass the Boards, work as an RN, and make money while finishing my Education degree. But life had other plans.

One semester, I was failing European History. I called my mother, who put my father on the phone. We weren't speaking at the time because he blamed my slipping grades on the Thursday night drinking I did with my friends. I planned to hang up on him, but I was too slow. I told him my situation, and he listened. I mean he really listened. Then he said, "I've never known you to quit anything. Why would you start now?"

I was furious and then I realized he was right. I stuck with the class and earned a B+. From then on, I stopped fighting him. He knew me better than I wanted to admit. I told him I loved him and meant it.

By the end of my second year, I realized I didn't want to be a teacher. I wanted to be a nurse. Nursing offered more flexibility, more opportunity, and, frankly, better pay. So I left CU and moved to Hartford, CT to live with my cousin while I worked as a secretary and nursing aide. That's also when I came out as gay. Soon after, I moved to Lambertville, New Jersey, and worked toward meeting prerequisites for the College of New Jersey. I was determined, and eventually, I was accepted.

I finished my BSN in two years. I worked as an RN, served as class president, and even led the graduation procession even though I accidentally led us down the wrong path. Only three other males were in my class, but we all got along.

Next, I entered Rutgers University's Psychiatric Nursing program. This was my true passion. It was demanding, intense, and transformative. Weekly clinical sessions involved taping an hour-long therapy session, transcribing it word-for-word, and processing it in front of classmates and supervisors. It was tough, but the support system there was the strongest I had ever known.

I worked full-time at Trenton Psychiatric Hospital while completing the program. One clinical experience taught me a lesson I've never forgotten. Sometimes you must slow down, "smell the roses," and really know your patient. The story of the mother seeking an exorcism for her son. This experience tested my faith, ethics, and creativity and remains one of the most unusual but formative moments of my early career.

During this time, I moved to New York City to live with Peter. We worked hard and played hard. These were the Kennedy years, and mental health initiatives funded much of my education. I commuted daily from NYC to Rutgers, working evenings at St. Vincent's Hospital. I graduated in 1980 but skipped the ceremony, choosing instead to spend the day on Fire Island. I regret that now.

After earning my master's, I worked in several NYC facilities. Eventually, I moved to Florida, then to Birmingham, Alabama, to pursue my doctorate at the University of Alabama at Birmingham (UAB). The program was rigorous, intellectually stimulating, and at times overwhelming. I designed my own Program of Study: Advanced Family Mental Health Nursing.

I was accused of cheating and I was eventually cleared. It shook me deeply. A closed-minded professor challenged me in another moment. But I learned resilience, courage, and the importance of standing firmly in my identity, especially when I openly shared that I was gay in a group discussion about sexuality.

My time at UAB was a blend of hard work, deep friendships, and enormous growth. My parents traveled from Vermont for my graduation, and I proudly introduced them to my faculty and friends.

The day after my doctorate ceremony was one of the hardest of my life. I woke up with nothing scheduled. I had no classes, no clinicals, no meetings and that made me feel utterly lost. It took several days to climb out of that emptiness. I realize now that I love to stay busy and struggle when I have days where there is nothing to do.

I later attempted additional study at NYU in Family Psychiatric Nursing but found the commute unmanageable. That marked the end of my formal academic pursuit; though not the end of my learning. Continuing education, workshops, and professional development carried me forward.

I used to believe life moved only when I pushed it forward; when I held on with white-knuckled determination. But adoption, loss, faith, and education taught me something gentler. Life also moves when you stop gripping so tightly. "Holding on" and "letting be" are not opposites; they are a rhythm.

Fear taught me to hold on. Faith taught me to loosen my grip.

Adoption gave me a beginning but left blank spaces. There were places where fear and hope lived side by side. Over the years, I learned to hold on to what steadied me and let be what I couldn't control. Faith carried me through the still places until, one ordinary day, stillness opened into revelation: I had the chance to learn where my story had truly begun.

In the end, the shape of knowing was never about discovering a single truth. It was about learning how to live inside the questions. It was about how to hold on, how to let go, and how to trust the quiet spaces where life continues to unfold.

And now I know:
Being still doesn't mean being lost.
Life happens, even when you stand still.
And sometimes, stillness is where hope finally begins.

Chapter 10

Defining Moments

After the winter semester ended at UAB, I decided to move to Washington, D.C. I'd always wanted to live in the nation's capital. I secured a job with the federal government as Director of Nursing Education for the National Institute of Mental Health at St. Elizabeths Hospital. The Neuropsychiatric Research Hospital (NRH) was a thirty-six bed research hospital focused solely on schizophrenia. I oriented new staff, provided ongoing education, worked on research procedures, wrote articles, gave presentations, and helped develop new measurement tools. Being surrounded by brilliant psychiatrists and researchers from around the world felt like working at the United Nations.

The hospital's mission was to find a treatment for schizophrenia. Even now, no cure exists. Parents would bring their loved ones with hope, and we often had to tell

them, "I'm sorry, but there is no cure yet."
There were many tears. In spite of
disappointments, I had to maintain hope for
patients, families, my staff, and myself.

One challenge of working in a research
hospital was that we couldn't use PRNs
(medications given as needed), because
they interfered with the integrity of the
studies. We relied solely on therapeutic
relationships. If a patient walked off the unit
and went to a bar, we couldn't physically
intervene. We had to talk them back. I was
proud of how my staff learned to listen,
engage, and build trust with these patients.

I felt deep empathy for people with
schizophrenia. A friend once said the
reason we don't understand them is
because they are more evolved than we
are, maybe even more advanced. After
many years living among them, I think he
may be right.

One patient once stopped me in the hallway
and said, with total seriousness but a smile
in his heart, "We've found the cure for

schizophrenia and the cure is cornbread!" I almost fell on the floor laughing.

Another morning, before I could even get out of my car, staff rushed to tell me that a patient had left the hospital. Since the doors weren't locked, he had simply walked off the unit, out the front door, across six lanes of interstate traffic, jumped a fence, and approached the President's helicopter. He wasn't doing anything wrong. He was just standing there. I spent the entire day with him through FBI, CIA, and White House interviews. My role was to protect him, not punish him. He was escorted back by police, and I went home exhausted but proud.

After I had been at NRH a few months, I noticed some nurses wearing uniforms that resembled Navy officers'. I learned they were part of the United States Public Health Service (USPHS). I joined and took an oath to defend the United States, saluting higher-ranking officers and learning mostly through mentorship. The Surgeon General is the lead officer of the Service, and it is an all-officer corps with no enlisted personnel.

Not long after joining, the Chief Nurse of NRH was removed, and I was asked to take over the position. It was my first high-level nursing administration job. Soon after, the Chief Nurse of the USPHS nominated me to serve as Advisor to the U.S. Surgeon General, C. Everett Koop, on Family Mental Health Issues. This was a tremendous honor. I wrote syllabi on family mental health concepts and taught other healthcare providers.

Defining moments rarely feel defined when they happen. Mine often felt like stumbles, doubts, or whispered prayers into the dark. Growing up adopted, I carried questions I was too afraid to ask, leaning on faith to steady the quiet trembling inside me. But when I finally reached the point of trying to find my birth family, I realized that every fear, every waiting season, every moment of stillness had been part of a larger story being written long before I knew how to read it.

I always liked work. I was never afraid of the challenges that came with it. I enjoyed earning money, saving it when I was younger, and spending it once I was old enough to appreciate the reward. I had a strong Protestant work ethic, and I liked having multiple jobs at once because I became bored easily. I think I inherited this from my mother, who always had another job in addition to working on the farm.

It began with small chores around the barn. I liked them, and I believed my father appreciated the extra help because it took pressure off the larger tasks.

My responsibilities increased as I got older, and I liked that. There was variety. Things like working in the garden, herding cattle in from the pastures, and tackling whatever needed to be done. One thing I didn't like was my father's reluctance to teach us about calving. He never wanted us to watch a cow give birth. One day, when he was away for his grain business, a cow began calving in the pasture while I was alone. I was terrified, not knowing what to do. When he returned, I told him he needed to let us watch so we could learn. He would show us anything except if it was related to sex.

The summer of my junior year, I worked at the Lakeview Inn near Caspian Lake in Greensboro, VT, as an assistant to the chef on Saturday evenings when they hosted their special meal. The lodge catered to "Summer Folks". These were wealthy families who lived elsewhere but arrived in Greensboro for the summer season.

Before college, I began my professional career as a secretary to the president of a rifle manufacturing company in Hartford, Connecticut. He was a wonderful and supportive boss with a great sense of humor. My responsibilities included ordering blueprints for rifles the company had manufactured elsewhere. I took dictation, typed letters, mailed them out, and filed copies. At first, two women assisted me, but after a few months I took on their tasks, and they resigned. I liked the job, but the idle hours became too much. I grew impatient and eventually resigned.

I heard about a job as a nurse's aide in the long-term care section of a Hartford hospital. It was my entry into nursing and the medical world. After several months, I learned of an opening in the emergency room. Craving excitement, I applied and got the job. I loved the pace, the new knowledge, and the variety. I met a nurse who had served in Vietnam and she took me under her wing. She let me take vital signs, conduct intake interviews, and work in the minor suture room cleaning trays. These were tasks I wouldn't have been allowed to do without her permission. Her support made me feel competent and raised my self-esteem. I woke each day looking forward to work.

My roommate had a friend who was Director of Financial Aid at The College of New Jersey (TCNJ). He told me there was financial assistance available for nursing students and encouraged me to apply. After persistent effort, I was admitted and received the aid I needed.

After moving to New Jersey and beginning my Bachelor's in Nursing, I passed my State Boards and worked as a Licensed Practical Nurse in a local nursing home. After completing my BSN at TCNJ, I entered Rutgers University for my master's degree and worked as a Registered Nurse at Trenton Psychiatric Hospital for three or four years.

While working on my MA, I moved to New York City and worked as a staff nurse at St. Elizabeth's Hospital in the West Village, then at the Bronx Veterans Medical Center. After finishing my MA, I became Head Nurse at New York Medical Center's Payne Whitney Clinic. I stayed there for four or five years until I moved to Florida to escape the stress and noise of NYC. I was ready for a calmer environment.

I accepted a position as a Psychiatric Clinical Nurse Specialist at the Orlando VA Outpatient Clinic. I was about to be granted prescriptive authority when I received my acceptance letter from the University of Alabama at Birmingham (UAB). I resigned from the VA and moved to Birmingham. Because the Birmingham VA had no psychiatric unit, I went to the Dean of the School of Nursing and asked if she had a job for me. She offered me an Assistant Professor position. This was my first teaching role. I was thrilled and anxious, but also unsure if I was ready. I had heard horror stories of long-time faculty losing their positions when they entered doctoral programs, so I felt fortunate. I stayed on for an extra semester after graduating and loved teaching. I realized I had wanted to be a nurse educator all my life.

I used to believe defining moments came with trumpet blasts. The clear signs would announce that life had changed. But mine often arrived quietly. The moment I first understood I was adopted was not dramatic. It felt like a soft click, like a small door unlocking. I didn't step through it then. I was too afraid but faith whispered that the door would wait. Years later, when I finally followed that whisper, I realized that every quiet moment of reckoning had prepared me for the possibility of meeting the family I never knew existed.

Before I even began to find a name or a face from my birth family, I found a moment that felt like standing on a diving board, toes curled over the edge. I didn't jump at first. Adoption had taught me to be cautious with dreams. Faith had taught me to wait. But life rarely waits with you. That moment, when I could no longer ignore the pull toward my own origins, became the turning point.

Defining moments often begin as whispers we try to silence. Mine started with a question: Who were the people who let me go? I swallowed it for years, afraid it would betray the family that raised me. But faith has a way of nudging truth forward. When I finally allowed myself to listen, I felt something open. It was a deep ache, but also a longing for my full story. The real defining moment wasn't a reunion. It was deciding to seek the truth, even when it scared me.

I always maintained a private practice on the side. I have worked evenings and Saturdays since my USPHS days. I loved the autonomy: being my own boss, hiring a team, and shaping the care. Running a practice requires discipline. In Princeton, New Jersey, I hired a psychiatrist, a social worker, and an office manager. Although I had never imagined myself owning a private practice, education and opportunity led me there. If something is deeply important, visualizing it makes it possible.

The hardest part of private practice was losing patients to suicide. Two of my patients died this way. The first was a young married man with an adopted son. The second was a young woman whom I mistakenly allowed to manipulate me into giving a thirty day supply of medication, which she consumed all at once. Only the person who succeeds truly knows why they choose suicide. I took responsibility. I grieved both losses deeply. Even now, I see their faces. These painful experiences taught me invaluable lessons and strengthened my skills with suicidal patients. I worked extensively with the first patient's wife and child, helping them grieve.

One of my patients, Carrie Van Ness, wrote about me in a testimonial:

> "There is one man, Dr. Ernest Lapierre, who has never disappointed me in life. He never refused to see me, even when I gave him many reasons to. I

would arrive at sessions in different cars, unable to stop myself. I took on too many activities and couldn't balance them. Though I became depressed, I never became suicidal. He diagnosed me with Bipolar Disorder, which explained everything, and always invited me into my treatment plan. There is no way to express my admiration or gratitude for this man. When I say one of a kind, I mean it." ~ *Carrie*

Her brother, Christopher Van Ness, also became my patient. He came at Carrie's urging after years of anger issues, learning disabilities, legal problems, and disillusionment with therapy. He told me he had asked his mother when his first therapy visit was, and she answered, "Third grade, when you tried to kill a nun."

He disliked every therapist he'd ever had, that is, until he met me. He said I was "the most amazing person" he'd ever spoken to in a therapeutic setting. I helped him confront issues with his father, his marriage, and suicidal thoughts. He made significant progress. He followed me from office to office, even across states. When an accident with an eighteen-wheeler ended his cooking career and his insurance stopped covering psychiatric care, I told him not to worry. We would keep working together. That meant a great deal to him.

I kept my private practice until I retired. I still miss it. I hoped to maintain it part-time in retirement, but scheduling, sessions, and billing became too cumbersome without staff support.

After moving to Vermont, I accepted online teaching positions with universities like Kaplan, teaching nursing courses. I enjoyed the mental stimulation but missed face-to-face engagement. Eventually I became Head of the Psychiatric Nursing Department at Norwich University, a mixed military and private school. I taught several courses, assisted in revising the nursing program, and built relationships with colleagues. I enjoyed my summers off.

My final position was Director of Education for the Vermont Psychiatric Care Hospital. I coordinated refresher courses like CPR, arranged training such as managing aggressive patients, and worked with a wonderful assistant and staff. I had an exceptional boss who supported my work. This job felt like the culmination of my career. It was the "swan song" that brought all my professional experiences together.

Professionalism, to me, means giving back to the profession that shaped you. That can be done by joining organizations like the American Nurses Association (ANA), National League for Nursing (NLN), or American Psychiatric Nurses Association (APNA). I would attend conferences, volunteer, write articles, and serve on editorial boards, as I did for APNA for six or seven years. These roles build community, leadership, and opportunity. They also bring joy. I still remember APNA meetings filled with long workdays followed by dinners and Broadway shows.

After leaving NIMH and while working at Washington Hospital, I connected with

Caitlyn Ryan, who was invited by Emory University to present on AIDS and Alcoholism. She asked me to collaborate. She also suggested including a young gay man living with both AIDS and alcoholism. He gladly agreed. I invited them to stay at my home in D.C., but Peter, my partner, was afraid of contracting AIDS. I explained that AIDS cannot be transmitted through casual contact, and after much discussion, he agreed. The young man stayed with us, and the presentation was a success.

I know it seemed like I changed jobs often, but doing so helped me understand what was out there. I discovered what I could aspire to and what roles might suit me. I constantly asked myself: "Is this something I want to be? How do they look? How do they act?" If no role models existed, I tried to be a trailblazer. If a job wasn't right, I learned to move on. I took positions I shouldn't have, and admitted it. When needed, I took breaks or less demanding roles until I was ready again.

Each defining moment carved space inside me, revealing a resilience I didn't know I had. These moments became guideposts. They were reminders that clarity often comes after confusion, and growth follows even the smallest shift. If life can change so profoundly in the still moments, I can only imagine what waits in the chapters ahead.

I used to fear the moments that pressed hardest against my life, thinking they would break me. Instead, they shaped me. They revealed the truths I needed in order to move at all. These defining moments. They were messy, tender, unexpected and became the compass I didn't know I was searching for. And as the dust settled, I realized that even in stillness, I had been quietly choosing who I wanted to be.

Chapter 11

The Meaning of Clarity

Clarity never arrived in my life as a single moment of revelation. It came slowly, like morning light stretching across a dark room, exposing what had always been there but what I had never fully dared to see. Growing up adopted, I lived between two stories. One I was given and one I could only imagine. Fear became a quiet shadow trailing behind me, teaching me to stay small; faith became the thin thread I clutched when the unknown felt too wide. For years, I believed clarity meant certainty, as if tracing my life back to its beginning could rewrite all the questions I had learned to live with. But clarity isn't certain. It's the willingness to open a door even when you're trembling on the threshold.

When I finally stepped forward, faith nudging me past the fear I'd mistaken for protection, I found not perfect answers but real faces which could be my birth family. People whose stories had been running parallel to mine, waiting for the day our lines might finally cross. Clarity revealed itself not as a destination, but as belonging, a truth that had been holding its breath until I was ready to meet it. In their voices, their names, and their familiar echoes of my own, I understood. Life happens even when you stand still, but clarity happens when you find the courage to move.

I never saw myself as a "common garden-variety drunk." My parents were strongly against alcohol. I never saw my mother take a sip, and the only time I ever saw my father lift a beer to his mouth, he didn't even drink it. He did it just to be polite to relatives.

My drinking began later than many of my friends. I was eighteen, newly graduated from high school, and working at the Lake View Inn on Caspian Lake in Greensboro, VT. On Saturday nights, after the big dinner service, the chef and I would sit, laugh, talk, and share a couple of cold beers. I hated the taste so much that I kept a Diet Coke in my other hand. I would take two sips of soda for every sip of beer to wash the taste away. The fact that I kept drinking it anyway should have been the first clue. Denial became my closest companion.

It wasn't long before someone from the inn would drive me to the bottom of our property, and then we'd switch seats so I could drive the rest of the way home. One night, I had an accident. I don't remember the details or how much damage there was or how I got out of trouble but alcohol was never considered the cause. Another time, I was so drunk I vomited between the wide floorboards in my bedroom. My sister blamed the drinking, but my mother refused to believe it and cleaned it up herself. Looking back, my mother was my strongest enabler.

Throughout that summer, I continued drinking on Friday and Saturday nights after work. I can't remember when I started buying my own alcohol, but I know it wasn't long afterward.

The first meetings I attended were held in the basement of a church. I had taken psychiatric patients to meetings before, but this was the first time I introduced myself as an alcoholic. I was told to find a sponsor and attend ninety meetings in ninety days.

My drinking worsened during my Master's program, though oddly, not during my doctoral studies. When I moved to Washington, DC, I was tired of being "sick and tired." I feared killing someone while driving drunk, so much so that I sold my white car and bought a red one because I didn't want the "blood to show" if something happened while I was driving drunk. That's how twisted my thinking had become.

During this time in my life, I wasn't sleeping. I often couldn't remember where I'd parked. One Saturday, I woke up at noon, which was early for me and called a friend named Caitlyn. I told her I thought I had a drinking problem. She listened, then said plainly, "Yes, you do. But with help, you can stop." I was relieved to hear someone tell me the truth.

She connected me with gay recovering alcoholics who took me to my first meeting.

They told me someone would meet me the next night and help me get started.

That date became my sobriety date: **Sunday, September 20, 1986**.

I had no idea if I would make it, but I held tightly to the saying, "One day at a time." One of my sponsors, Dennis, used to joke, "In these meetings, you go upstairs to save your soul and downstairs to save your ass!"

For the first time in a long while, I felt safe. Denial was over. Thank God!

I briefly considered entering rehab. I scheduled an intake interview at Whitman-Walker Clinic, a leader in LGBTQ+ recovery services. The counselor was thirty minutes late and took three personal calls during my appointment. I was so angry and disappointed by how dismissive he was that I never went back. Instead, I chose to remain sober through meetings and support from my community. I also knew I couldn't afford anger if I wanted to stay sober.

During this time of intense change, I became overwhelmed and confused.

Thoughts of suicide surfaced, and I knew I needed help to stay safe. I admitted myself to the psychiatric unit at Georgetown University Hospital for a week. I received evaluations, alcoholism counseling, medication, and set up outpatient psychiatric care and rehabilitation sessions.

My sponsor visited often and took me to meetings almost every evening. I held on tightly to the support around me and that community helped save my life.

Sobriety anniversaries became deeply meaningful to me and became more important than birthdays. My first one felt like a miracle. Staying sober for a full year once seemed impossible, but there I was, celebrating it.

I learned I could enjoy celebrations sober. I enjoyed dances, New Year's Eve parties, and gatherings with friends. After ten or eleven years of sobriety, I entered a dark and confusing time in my life. I wasn't proud of this.

I remember one morning standing on a street corner waiting to cross to the other side. There were a couple of men dressed in leather on the side of the street and a little boy, about seven or eight standing on the other side of the street with his mother. All of a sudden out of nowhere I heard the little boy ask his mother why those men were dressed in leather? His mother told him without any hesitation that part of this behavior was because they liked the feel of the leather. I thought that was such a good answer on her part.

I liked the fantasy that sadomasochism offered with the leather outfits of pants, shirts and coats, a hat and black boots. My uniform consisted of jeans, a T-shirt, and sneakers, no hat. There were the very masculine men, who wore leather shirts, jackets, pants, boots and hats. I tended to be more feminine myself although I often switched between the different roles of sadomasochism or when a person derives pleasure from experiencing pain, or suffering themselves. This person may enjoy being dominated or controlled by others. Masochism can be a form of self-punishment as a way of coping with difficult emotions.

A sadist is a person who derives pleasure from inflicting pain, humiliation or suffering on others. This person is often characterized by a lack of empathy, a desire to control and may engage in abusive or violent behaviors.

I was also surprised that I didn't find someone with difficult emotions like mine such as a masochist to be my guide into the journey of sadomasochism. I do know that I was getting older and trusting myself to be able to just venture out into the unknown by myself and be safe. That is why I felt that I didn't need Peter to go with me on this journey. In fact I really wanted to go on this journey by myself so I did proceed all alone. I did know that there was an element of safety and danger in sadomasochism involving procedures like whips, chains, handcuffs and others. I really hadn't done any research or studied sadomasochism, or talked with anyone about what sadomasochism entailed or was all about. I had seen men in leather outfits in bars and even out on the streets in broad daylight and I knew they were into sadomasochism even though I didn't talk with them. I also knew right from the start that leather was something that I wasn't or probably never would be into wearing. I remember that when I was into sadomasochism, it was more standard for a Sadist to wear leather while more common for a Masochist to wear jeans, a T-shirt and black boots. Oftentimes both men in the couple were a combination and wore leather also. There were sadomasochism Clubs that I could have gone to where I could talk with members about what sadomasochism was all about. But I was too afraid to enter them and approach someone who was a complete stranger.

I do recall that I couldn't wait to go to my first sadomasochism bar. I remember that this event like it was yesterday. I walked in the door all by myself, and thought that all eyes were on me. It was like I was a new piece of meat, which turned out to be true. The feeling was much like that first night in the gay bar as well. Leaning up against a wall with a beer in one hand, waiting for someone to come along and talk to me. My trepidation with the idea forced me to go very slowly to get into sadomasochism in any depth. I had heard things by this time, and I was very afraid of getting hurt. I was very sure that it wasn't going to happen because I knew that now I had a firm handle on saying no and meaning just that. The only thing that concerned me was being restrained in some way and not being able to stop the use of pain inflicting devices. The only thing I knew that would work was not to allow myself to be restrained in any form in the first place. I did have some concerns because of how small I am. I had learned from past experiences that sometimes a soft voice gets far greater results than a loud threatening one.

Welts and black and blue marks inflicted by chains, whips, paddles and hands, often made it impossible to take off my clothes. This was especially true in a public place or trying to wear a bathing suit for many years. I lived in fear that someone might see them and ask me where they came from. Ironically, as far as I was concerned, they were often inflicted, from the need to feel alive and loved. This felt much like the attempts to commit suicide were and are still today when they come on.

Verbal humiliation was a big part of sadomasochistic behavior. While this seemed to fit into my personal persona, from many years of my past life, there were many times that this occurred in private and in public. I remember one guy who verbally humiliated me, by berating me, just because I refused to choose the restaurant for us to go to that Saturday evening. I knew from past experiences that not making the choice of restaurants wouldn't have mattered because no matter what restaurant I chose I would have gotten berated if not slapped in the face anyway. I recall that this easily fit into my persona as an individual who had such low self-esteem for many years.

I didn't get close to any of the men I met during this period of my life and I was satisfied with my relationship with Peter. I became happier just with life the way life was and decided to leave my life that way. I know that this was a good decision even today. I couldn't think of anything else new that I wanted to put into my life. At least I was satisfied for a good long time with keeping things the way they were. Something I hadn't been for my life in some time, but this decision really felt good.

Am I glad I took the journey into Sadomasochism when there were other journeys I could have taken? I sure am. If I hadn't taken this one to this day I would be wondering just exactly what this lifestyle was like. I went and did the exploring for myself and got the picture first hand, and out of my system. I no longer have to ask myself what am I missing.

One thing that I regretted a lot doing with my journey into sadomasochism but have lived in denial about this thing until recently when someone brought this idea to my attention, is the fact that all the time I was into sadomasochism, I was actually cheating on Peter. I accept now that Peter didn't like that I got into sadomasochism very much. I think it was because he was very afraid that I would somehow or someway get hurt and he didn't want to see that happen to me. Peter was very protective of me and I appreciated that about him. While Peter never wanted to step in the way of my discovering anything I wanted to, I think he would have been much more at ease if I had found some sadomasochists and vicariously gone through the experience by talking to them. I felt very guilty and sorry for having put Peter through my journey and although I am glad that I did the journey by myself, I often wished I didn't put him through it.

On September 20,2025, I celebrated 39 years of sobriety. I think that is nothing short of a miracle and this group of people who have helped millions of people get and stay sober for years has helped me be successful in this journey.

I am so glad that I have never had to struggle with the desire of not taking a drink in my history of sobriety. I recall that the same thing happened with me about stopping smoking and stopping biting my nails. I don't know what there is about me that this happens, that when I get ready to stop something I just stop that thing, but I sure am happy that for me things happen that way.

As my life continued to unfold, I learned unexpected lessons in recovery. One was discovering that I didn't like groups or speaking in them. A woman, who later became my wife, once stopped me after a meeting and said, "It was so good to hear you talk. I thought you were mute!" From then on, I didn't stay silent. I began sharing, and eventually saw how my story might help someone else.

I also learned I could walk into a liquor store again without fear. I never imagined that this would be possible. My sponsor dragged me in one day without warning. It wasn't nearly as frightening as I'd expected.

As time went on, I lost the ability to drive, which made attending meetings more difficult. I relied on old friends, former sponsors, and members of my home group to help me get there. When I attended meetings, I'd introduce myself and ask if anyone could offer rides that accommodated my walker. People always stepped up.

Zoom meetings became another lifeline. With time zones spanning the globe, I could attend a meeting any hour of the day.

It was also through meetings that I met the woman I married. She had four daughters and a young son. I loved her children as it provided me with an instant family. We were living in a rented house with her ex-lover at the time, which was unusual, but it worked. Eventually her ex found a partner and moved out. Our wedding was simple: matching white T-shirts, jeans, sneakers, a Justice of the Peace, breakfast afterward, and then everyone went to work and school. No honeymoon needed.

We had several good years together. I felt proud as the breadwinner. But eventually, the stress of family demands grew too heavy. Divorce, which was something I had never wanted, became unavoidable. My instinct was to run, but my lawyer warned me that leaving would count as abandonment. Mary Ellen gave me an amicable divorce, and I remain grateful for that. It was the first of three divorces in my life.

I packed an eighteen-wheeler almost entirely by myself and drove it alone to Lambertville, New Jersey. It was Easter weekend. Most of my friends were away. I managed to move all by myself.

Through all of it, including the stress, transitions, and heartbreak, I never took a drink. Not once. Drinking simply wasn't an option anymore.

Clarity, I've learned, isn't something you find all at once. It arrives in pieces, sometimes quietly, sometimes after years of feeling lost. For much of my life, I felt suspended between stories. I was adopted but searching, sober but rebuilding, afraid but moving anyway. I thought I needed answers to feel whole, but what I really needed was the courage to keep going.

Clarity didn't erase my past. It helped me understand it. It showed me that belonging can take more than one shape, and that family can come to you in different seasons of your life. It taught me that stillness isn't failure. It's often the space where truth gathers strength before revealing itself.

Trying to find my birth parents didn't complete me, but it expanded me. Sobriety didn't fix everything, but it gave me the ground I needed to stand on. Each part of my story was messy, complicated, beautiful and has shown me something about who I am.

And that, more than anything, is what clarity has become:
 not certainty, but understanding.
 Not perfection, but presence.
 Not answers, but awareness.

Chapter 12

Two Sides of the

Same Coin

I have always thought of myself as a physically healthy person, that is, until my later years. I had all my childhood vaccinations and have kept up with them even today.

I used to believe that life moved only when I moved with it, that standing still meant being left behind. But adoption taught me early that life has a rhythm all its own. The rhythm was one that I didn't always feel ready for. Fear lived quietly in the corners of my childhood, whispering questions about who I was and where I belonged. Yet faith threaded through those uncertainties, steady even when I was not. When I finally set out to find my birth family, I realized the answers waiting for me were not separate from the life I'd been living, but simply the other side of the same coin.

Growing up adopted meant learning to hold two truths at once: gratitude and grief, hope and fear, belonging and longing. I spent years trying to choose which side to live on, as if one would cancel out the other. Instead, I became an expert at standing still, trying not to disturb the life I'd been given while secretly wondering about the life I'd lost. Faith kept tugging at my sleeve, urging me to trust what I couldn't yet see. When I finally went searching for my birth family, I discovered that the story I feared would shatter me was actually the one that made me whole.

Adoption asked me to build a life on a foundation I hadn't chosen. Fear told me not to ask questions. Faith insisted I'd survive the answers. For years, I lived between those voices, suspended in a kind of stillness that felt safe but never settled. Then came the day I decided to look for my birth family. It was a decision that cracked open everything I thought I understood about myself. What I found was not just a new chapter, but the matching face of a coin I'd carried my whole life.

From the outside, my life looked calm. It had steady routines, familiar faces, a practiced smile for every uncertain moment. But inside, adoption planted a restlessness that no amount of stillness could quiet. I lived with questions that curled around my faith, tugging at its edges, testing its strength. When fear told me to stay put, faith nudged me forward. And so I stepped into the search for my birth family, discovering that life had been moving toward this moment long before I dared to follow.

I used to picture my life as a coin tossed into the air. On one side etched with the family that raised me, the other side with the family I'd never known. For years, I watched it spin, afraid to see which side would land facing up. Adoption had given me love, but it had also given me questions I wasn't sure I had the courage to answer. Faith became the quiet hand reaching out beneath that spinning coin. When I finally looked for my birth family, I learned that both sides of my story had always belonged to me.

When I was in seventh or eighth grade, I wanted to try out for some sports teams, so I had to take a physical. I went to see a local doctor in Hardwick, VT. My mother let me go into his office by myself while she stayed in the waiting room. This was a very grown-up action for her to take, as it was the first time she hadn't accompanied me to a doctor's visit. I remember feeling proud that I was growing up.

Once in his office, I took off my clothes. The doctor asked, "Do you know that you had rickets as a child?" He explained:

"Rickets is a childhood disorder where bones soften, weaken, and become prone to fractures and deformity due to inadequate calcium and phosphate in the body, most commonly from a prolonged vitamin D deficiency. This deficiency hinders the absorption of essential minerals needed for bone formation, leading to symptoms like bone pain, muscle weakness, poor growth, bowed legs, and dental problems. While nutritional rickets from low vitamin D is most common, other causes include calcium or phosphate deficiency, and rare genetic

forms that affect how the body handles these minerals."
(www.mayoclinic.org/diseases-conditions/rickets/symptoms-causes/syc-20351943)

I told him I had never noticed any bowing in my legs. He explained that rickets can cause leg bones to bow away from the center of the body. Then he asked if I wanted him to break all the bones in my lower legs, the fibula and tibia, and reset them so they would be straight. I said no. Then, trying to make a joke, I asked if I could turn around and break his legs instead. He just looked at me as if I had two heads.

I told my mother what had happened, and she just laughed. She said she wasn't surprised because she knew how precocious I was.

I also remember contracting measles around the time of that physical. I didn't know I had it and went merrily off to 4-H Summer Camp, unknowingly bringing the infection with me. Many children had to leave early and go home, just as my mother had had to come pick me up. I didn't win the Most Valuable Camper award that year, and I felt guilty for causing other campers to miss out on an experience they had anticipated all year.

I had a tonsillectomy as a junior in high school. I kept coughing and tore the stitches, so I had to return to the operating room to have them redone under anesthesia. I had an uneventful appendectomy around age sixteen.

Growing up adopted meant living with two versions of myself. One version I carried proudly, and one I kept buried under years of quiet fear. For so long, I believed standing still would keep those fears from catching up with me. It was the fear of not belonging, fear of asking questions, fear of hoping for answers. Yet life has a way of moving for us. Even when I stood frozen, faith tugged me forward. Sometimes it was a gentle tug and sometimes with a force I didn't understand. When the moment came to search for my birth family, the coin flipped. On one side stood the boy who had learned to survive in silence; on the other, the man willing to step into truth. Both were me and both were finally ready to meet.

Adoption placed a coin in my hands before I could speak. It was a symbol of two beginnings, two stories, two unknowns. One side was the life I was given, full of love but shadowed by questions I was taught not to ask. The other side shimmered with mystery, its image worn smooth from years of wondering. Fear kept me gripping that coin too tightly, afraid to flip it. But faith whispered that standing still wasn't the same as being safe. I finally released my grip. The coin spun, catching light from every direction, and when it landed, I found myself staring into the faces of my birth family. These were the people who shaped the half of me I'd never allowed myself to see. Life had happened while I stood still, and finally, I chose to move with it. For most of my life, I thought being adopted meant I should be endlessly grateful. I should be grateful enough not to question, not to search, not to feel afraid. But fear grew in the quiet spaces my gratitude couldn't fill. There were two versions of me. One version anchored in the family who raised me and another drifting in the unknown, tethered only by faith that someday I'd understand where I truly came from. When I finally chose to look for my birth family, it felt like both betrayal and salvation. That's the thing about two sides of the same coin. They're inseparable, no matter how different. I learned that I didn't have to choose between them. I only had to be brave enough to hold both.

Life has a way of moving you even when you swear you're standing still. Adoption taught me early that some answers would never be mine, so I stopped reaching for them. But fear never went away; it simply settled in, becoming part of my routine, like breath I didn't think about. Faith was the only thing that kept me from shutting down altogether. It was a quiet reminder that unseen paths still lead somewhere. When I finally opened the door to finding my birth family, I stepped into a truth that had been waiting for me all along. Two sides of who I am came face-to-face, and for the first time, I felt the weight of my life balance instead of tip.

While I was still living in Hartford, Connecticut, I worked at a rifle manufacturing firm as secretary to the president. I became bored quickly, and my efficiency accidentally eliminated two positions. I wanted out. I considered hospital work and eventually got a job at the old Hartford Hospital in the rehabilitation unit. The work, mostly with elderly patients nearing the end of life, was meaningful, but not the right fit for me. When a job opened in the Emergency Room, I took it. I loved the pace, the intensity, and the sense of purpose.

Not long after, I was recruited to assist with minor surgical procedures, and I found that I took to the surgical suite naturally. Then one day, as I walked down the ER hallway, a doctor friend pulled me into the men's room. He asked how many times I had shot up that week. Shocked, I denied ever doing drugs and demanded to know why he was asking. He told me to look in the mirror. My eyes and skin were yellow. He examined me and diagnosed me with Hepatitis B. He ordered me home to Vermont to rest for two weeks. I recovered fully and returned to work, grateful to be back in the ER where I felt competent and proud.

Around age 22 or 23, after moving from Hartford to Trenton, New Jersey, I came out as gay and also discovered my strong sexual appetite. I wasn't discreet about choosing partners, and I found myself dealing with recurring sexually transmitted infections. I remember the embarrassment of walking into the New Jersey Department of Health clinic. The staff was always kind and discreet, but I still felt dirty and foolish, especially as someone entering the nursing profession. It seemed like every month I was back again with another infection.

The treatment was a painful penicillin injection given with a large, old-fashioned needle that sometimes had a burr. This was a sharp imperfection that made the shot hurt even more. I often thought the pain alone should have stopped my behavior. The counselors talked to me about safer choices. They never shamed me. They simply taught me. Eventually the lessons sank in, and once I began choosing partners more carefully, the infections stopped.

Years later, I developed a bladder condition that caused bright yellow or orange urine and required me to urinate very frequently. I learned to map out bathrooms everywhere I went and wore protective briefs to avoid accidents. It was embarrassing at first, but I realized I only owed explanations when I wanted to give them.

At 57, during a routine check-up, my doctor discovered I was having a heart attack. I was admitted to the ICU, and by the next morning, my heart converted back to a normal rhythm on its own. I've been stable on medication ever since.

I had ignored clear signs of the heart attack, convinced I could sleep it off. My doctor later told me bluntly how dangerous that had been. I promised I would never ignore those symptoms again.

I've had long stretches of wellness in my life, and I'm grateful for them. At 76, wellness feels different. It is more like periods *between* illnesses. This past year I was diagnosed with Parkinson's disease, though it appeared on my medical record before anyone told me. I had suspected it for years. My tremors, especially in my right hand, made eating messy at times, and I've had several serious falls that I use a walker now.

I lost my driver's license five years ago after falling asleep at the wheel. The walker makes driving impossible anyway. Being unable to get around on my own has been one of the hardest adjustments. I try to replace every loss with something I can still control. I like keeping my own schedule, putting away my laundry, and maintaining small routines that make me feel grounded.

My hearing loss requires hearing aids that continue to be adjusted as my hearing worsens. Hearing loss can make isolation feel easier than socializing, but I've learned to ask people to repeat themselves rather than pretend I heard them. It signals that I care enough to stay connected.

I also struggle with vision problems. Cloudiness and difficulty reading small print led me to my ophthalmologist, who eventually diagnosed ptosis, which is a drooping eyelid caused by aging muscles. Now I use adhesive strips each morning to lift my lids, and they've made reading possible again.

About four years ago, I moved into the Craftsbury Community Care Center, a retirement community that I love. I have enough space, my own furnishings, and support for everything except my daily living activities. I enjoy group exercises, activities, and the interdependence the community fosters. I believe that if you don't use your mind and body, you lose them.

Aging means giving up things like driving, or doing certain tasks independently but not everything has to be a loss. I've rediscovered reading and puzzles, which keep my mind sharp. I've learned that asking others for help creates connection rather than dependence.

There are very few people I can't get along with, but when I met a doctor who treated me dismissively and ignored my hearing loss, I eventually fired her. I don't believe anyone has to tolerate being treated as less than human.

Five or six years ago, I was volunteering for "Breakfast on Us," a program feeding people who were homeless or struggling. This was at the church I attended in Morrisville, VT. I loved the work. It made me feel useful and connected. Then one morning I fell asleep at the wheel and crashed head-on into a milk truck. No one was hurt, but my car was totaled, and I never drove again. I had to give up the volunteer work I loved, which was a painful loss.

Around 2024, during the COVID years, I began falling frequently and losing interest in everything. I slept almost constantly, stopped caring about hygiene, and struggled even with my walker. EMTs were called more than once. My niece Tracy and my case manager, Kelly, became concerned enough to review my advance directives. My life seemed to move in peaks and valleys. Sometimes I felt like myself again, and sometimes it felt like everything had collapsed. Kelly reminded me that the support around me and careful changes to my medications, had brought me back before and likely would again.

Recently, worsening vision brought me back to my ophthalmologist, who confirmed the diagnosis of ptosis and helped me find treatment that restored my ability to read small print. It was another reminder not to ignore what my body tells me.

Looking back, I see clearly that someone else has often been in the driver's seat when I couldn't be. I'm grateful for that.

I learned that my body has always told the truth, even when I didn't want to listen. I learned that asking for help doesn't diminish me. It connects me. I learned that losing abilities doesn't mean losing purpose. Sometimes it just means finding new ways to show up in the world. And I learned that the people who step in when I'm struggling are often the reason I find my way back.

Life happened in moments big and small, frightening and ordinary. Even when I thought I was standing still, something was shifting, teaching me, or surprising me. And maybe that's enough. Simply noticing that I'm still here, still learning, still moving forward.

Chapter 13

Holding On, Letting Go

I used to believe life moved only when I pushed it forward—when I held tight to the reins, knuckles white with determination. But somewhere between being adopted, losing my footing, and learning to trust in something larger than my fear, I discovered another truth: life happens even when you stand still. "Holding on" and "letting be" became less of a contradiction and more of a rhythm. It was one that eventually led me back to the people whose faces I had only ever imagined.

If you had asked me years ago, I would have said I survived by holding on. I was busy clutching at certainty, safety, and whatever scraps of control I could gather. That's what fear teaches you. But faith, in its quiet way, teaches something else. It whispers that sometimes the only way forward is to stop gripping so tightly. I didn't know it then, but releasing my fear is what opened the door to the moment I finally searched for my birth family.

My earliest memories are stitched together with both comfort and questions. Adoption gave me a beginning, but it also left spaces. The spaces were silent places where fear lived alongside hope. As the years unfolded, I learned how to hold on to what steadied me and let be what I couldn't control. Faith carried me across the still places, the waiting places, until one ordinary day became extraordinary. I was hopeful for the day I learned where my story had truly begun.

There is a peculiar stillness that settles in when you've spent your life searching for something you're not sure you'll ever find. I lived much of my life in that stillness. I was afraid to disturb it, afraid it might swallow me whole. Adoption taught me both belonging and longing; faith kept me from unraveling. Yet it wasn't until I surrendered that the search for my birth family could finally appear, like a constellation suddenly visible in a night sky I thought I already knew.

Faith has a way of asking us to loosen our grip on the world, on our fears, our stories, and even our identities. For most of my life, I held on anyway, afraid that letting go would erase what little I understood about who I was. Adoption blessed me and bewildered me in equal measure. But somewhere between the stillness and the struggle, grace found an opening. And through that opening walked the answers I had been unknowingly waiting for.

I've spent years learning the art of staying still, of listening for the truth beneath the noise of fear. Adoption shaped me, faith steadied me, and yet a part of me always drifted toward the questions I pretended not to ask. Holding on kept me safe; letting me be set me free. And in the quiet that followed, I was finally ready to hear the footsteps of the people whose stories were tied to mine from the beginning.

My problems with mental illness began when I was about 10 or 11. One night, I woke up and couldn't get back to sleep. I felt depressed, although I didn't know what to call it. I knew my mother gave us kids Aspirin for anything that ailed us, so I decided to take some. I thought that if one was good, many would be better. I ended up taking the whole bottle.

I didn't think much of it until I got to school and began to feel sick with an upset stomach. I told Mrs. Lee, my favorite teacher, what I had done. She called my mother, who came, brought me home, and put me to bed. This was a pattern of care that followed me for many years. This event was never referred to as a suicide attempt. How would someone so young know that a full bottle of Aspirin could be lethal? From my perspective, I just wanted to feel better and get some sleep. Suicide certainly would have provided that sleep, though.

No other suicide attempts occurred that I remember until the summer between my first and second years at Castleton State College. I was taking a required course in Psychiatric Nursing at the Brattleboro Retreat, a well-known psychiatric hospital in lower Vermont. During supper, the residents put on a show of cutting themselves with knives to unnerve us students. That scene haunted me. I couldn't sleep that night.

The next day, during clinical practice in a unit, I felt anxious and uncomfortable around "these types" of patients. I told my instructor about my thoughts and feelings, and she arranged for me to see the psychiatrist on call. He assessed me, gave me a small prescription to calm down, and scheduled an appointment for the next morning. I was staying with relatives in Brattleboro, and when I saw him the next day, I became agitated and took all the remaining pills in his office.

I remember sitting there, wondering why he didn't continue therapy or find someone else to help me. My mother came again to take me home, feed me, and put me to bed. I knew she didn't fully understand what I had done, but I couldn't understand why she or the psychiatrist wouldn't ensure I received more help. I was too ashamed to ask for help. I was so tired, and confused.

Why didn't I ask my father? He seemed distant from the situation. I don't remember him leaving work to talk to me. I felt invisible, though perhaps this was only my interpretation.

I had a love-hate relationship with mental illness. I knew I wasn't doomed because I had attempted suicide, but I was angry that I had to deal with this, alongside other challenges. At least I had a name for what was happening. At the same time, I hated the stigma and wanted to deny that mental illness existed for me. I wanted to hide it from everyone.

I also have a love-hate relationship with others' struggles with mental illness, for the same reasons. I believe there's a point of no return in suicidal thoughts. It is a threshold beyond which recovery becomes much harder. I liken it to a light switch. Once you flip the switch, the energy it creates continues until the switch is turned off. You "win" over suicide if the part of you that wants to live is stronger than the part that wants to end life.

I was misdiagnosed early on with only depression when I actually had bipolar disorder, which is a chronic mental health condition marked by extreme mood swings between mania and depression. Mania involves elevated mood, racing thoughts, rapid speech, decreased need for sleep, inflated self-esteem, and impulsivity. Depression brings persistent sadness, fatigue, lack of interest, feelings of worthlessness, and thoughts of suicide. Bipolar disorder was once called manic depression.

I experienced more depression than mania, though I did have periods of intense rage, which is a sign of mania. The most significant mania occurred around age forty-five, when I spent $3,000–$4,000 on clothes in a couple of days. I wasn't on medication or therapy at the time. I never had another episode like that, likely because I resumed treatment and never stopped.

I have to admit, I loved the euphoria of mania. Floating on a cloud, I feared the inevitable crash into depression and possibly suicidal thoughts or behaviors.

I've tried many treatments for mental illness, from medications with terrible side effects to those that brought restfulness, anxiety relief, and better sleep. Some treatments seemed preposterous, like waking up from a suicide attempt in an ER in New Jersey to find a policeman standing by my bed with a loaded revolver.

There's a peculiar fear in not knowing where you started. It followed me through childhood and into adulthood, whispering questions I never fully answered. I learned to live around it, careful not to press too hard on the tender parts. Adoption was both my anchor and my mystery. For a long time, I mistook stillness for safety. I stood so perfectly still that even searching for my birth family felt like a betrayal to my parents, myself, and the fragile balance I had built.

But life moves even when you refuse to. Faith nudged me. It was a gentle stirring, like someone knocking from inside a locked door. When I finally searched, it wasn't bravery but exhaustion that carried me forward. I believed that the day I would be able to hear my birth family's voices, something inside me would loosen. It wasn't a clean break or a cinematic epiphany. It was a quiet release. It was a sense that letting go of old fears didn't mean losing myself; it meant meeting myself, perhaps for the first time.

I had odd ways of coping, like giving my suicidal thoughts a name, Ralph, and talking to him. This personification helped me distance myself from the urge to act. I would even imagine a Board of Directors in my head to vote on decisions I couldn't make alone, with the Chairman as the final decision-maker.

Sometimes I heard frightening voices telling me I wasn't worth anything or instructing me on how to kill myself. I strongly encourage anyone experiencing this to seek help immediately. Call your local Crisis Hotline; in the U.S., dial 988.

I have been in therapy since childhood and continue today, currently on an every other week schedule. I value the relationship I cultivate with my therapist, carefully considering what I want to discuss before each session. Therapy has been a lifeline.

I've been on nearly every psychotropic medication from the late seventies through today. Some were helpful; others made me feel like a zombie. I currently take medication that works for me, with careful oversight from my psychiatrist. Modern treatment teams involve the patient and often family members, making care far more collaborative than in the past.

I pioneered home mental health visits, which allowed me to see patients in their own environments. These visits revealed realities that patients couldn't or wouldn't share in an office setting. A cup of tea, a cookie, and a gentle touch could make a patient well until the next visit. Safety was always paramount. Once, a delusional patient tried to attack me, and I called 911 to ensure her and my safety.

Holding on and letting go are not opposites. They are partners in the same dance. Adoption taught me to cling to questions I didn't yet have words for, and faith taught me to release them before they crushed me. Standing still didn't mean being stuck; it meant allowing life to gather courage around me. When I began the search for my birth family, I realized I hadn't been waiting alone. Something larger than fear had been guiding me all along, preparing me not just to receive answers but to belong.

All my life, I had held on to the fear that I was searching for something that might not want to be found. Letting go of that fear felt like stepping into thin air, trusting that faith would catch me. And it did. Life happens, even when you stand still, is more than a lesson. It was my reality. Finding my birth family wouldn't erase the ache of the years before, but it softened the edges. It could show me that love can travel distances we can't measure, and that sometimes, while we are standing still, a home we've never known is already making its way toward us.

My life has been a tapestry of holding tight to the threads I understood and loosening my grip on those woven in mystery. In adoption, I learned to cherish the unseen hand that guided me. In fear, I learned what it meant to tremble and still keep moving. In faith, I found the courage to stand still when the world around me kept shifting. And then, gracefully and unexpectedly, the pattern shifted. I looked forward to seeing the faces that mirrored mine. I might find my birth family. I understood. Letting go did not mean losing anything. It had simply cleared the way for everything I had been waiting for.

If this chapter has taught me anything, it's that life rarely follows the plans we sketch in our minds. I spent years holding on to hopes too delicate to speak aloud, and just as many letting go of fears that tried to rewrite my story. Through adoption, through stillness, through faith, I grew into someone who could finally reach for the truth. And when I began the search for my birth family, the ground beneath me shifted. It wasn't violently, but like a door quietly opening after a lifetime of knocking. It reminded me that even when nothing seems to be moving, something always is. Sometimes, it's us.

Chapter 14

The Faith I Inherited

In writing *Life Happens, Even When You Stand Still*, I've come to understand that the quietest moments often carry the loudest truths. The faith I inherited is not the kind passed down through bloodlines I never knew, but the kind stitched into me through uncertainty, hope, and the ache of wondering who I belonged to. Adoption taught me early that fear can shadow even the brightest rooms but faith has a way of pulling a chair beside you anyway. And when I finally decided to look for my birth family, I realized that faith had been leading me there long before I knew the path existed.

In the story I tell here, nothing has stood more still or moved more fiercely than the faith I inherited. It steadied me when fear felt like a second skin, held me through nights filled with questions about where I came from and why I was given away. Adoption gave me a beginning, but faith carried me forward. And it was faith that was stubborn and unshakable that finally led me to search for the family I had thought about for all my life.

The faith I inherited didn't arrive as a gift wrapped in heritage or family stories. It came from learning to trust life even when I felt too afraid to move. For years I stood still. I was terrified of searching and terrified of not searching. But faith nudged me forward in ways I didn't recognize at the time. And as I stepped toward the unknown, I found the people who helped me find the missing pieces of myself.

Faith rests at the heart of this memoir. It is the faith that lives under layers of fear, doubt, and longing that adoption quietly creates. For years I was afraid to look back, unsure of what I might find. But faith, persistent as a heartbeat, kept urging me on.

For clarity, religion can be understood as "an organized system of beliefs, practices, and rituals centered on a transcendent power or deity" (Austin, 2021). Spirituality, on the other hand, is "a broader concept encompassing an individual's search for meaning and connection with something greater than oneself, which may or may not be tied to a formal religion" (Austin, 2021). It is possible, and often enriching, to be both religious and spiritual.

Religion can be viewed as working from the outside in, whereas spirituality often works from the inside out. I have always thought of myself as a religious person. I remember my mother holding me in her arms and taking me to services before I could even recall them. That memory brings me a feeling of closeness, peace, and love I deeply needed.

Sundays in my home followed a routine. Breakfast was right after morning chores. Then the entire family attended the church service. We enjoyed socializing when we were old enough and then we returned home to a dinner simmered on the old iron stove. That routine, simple as it was, brought comfort and structure. As I grew, I participated in Sunday School, Youth Group, Choir, and even considered becoming a minister during high school. Life took me on a winding path, exploring multiple denominations, and eventually brought me to a church close to my home where I participated fully by attending services, Bible studies, and community events.

Prayer has been a cornerstone of my faith. I pray for guidance, healing, and gratitude. I pray at sunrises next to my window in my room that faces east and again at the sunsets to the west. I also quietly pray in my heart throughout the day. Faith is not just a practice. It is a relationship with yourself and God. Though I now walk with the assistance of a walker, it hasn't stopped me from attending church or seeking connection with God.

Spirituality complements this faith. Meditation, nature, poetry, music, and listening to others bring me grounding and purpose. I strive to give back, to act without expectation of return, and to help others where I can. Faith and spirituality, for me, are not rules to follow but lifelines that connect me to something larger than myself.

Growing up, I believed the faith I inherited came packaged neatly with my adoption papers. It included a new name, a new home, and a family who prayed over every fear I didn't yet have words for. But faith, I learned, doesn't always grow quietly in the background. Sometimes it trembles. Sometimes it hides. And sometimes it feels like standing still in the middle of a life that keeps unfolding without your permission. When the time came to search for my birth family, the old fear returned. The fear of knowing and the fear of not knowing were there but beneath it was a deeper pull. I had inherited a faith that whispered, *Keep going. Even stillness has a direction.* And so I followed.

By adulthood, faith had become both my anchor and my question mark. Adoption taught me how to cling to what I was given, even while wondering what I had lost. I lived in a kind of spiritual quiet. I was present, but paused, waiting for something unnamed to shift. Fear was my constant companion, but faith rose in response, steadily, quietly, until the first clue of my birth family. In that moment, faith met truth, and I understood that seeking where I came from wasn't betrayal. It was believing that God could hold all the pieces of me at once.

Faith is not a destination; it is the courage to open the next door. If I found my birth family, it wouldn't rewrite my story. It might complete a circle that faith had been drawing long before I understood its shape. My adoption, my fears, my searching, they were all chapters of the same story, held together by the belief that life keeps unfolding even when I stand still. Faith didn't give me all the answers, but it gave me the strength to ask the questions. And that strength led me home.

Looking back, I see now that every step, every fear, every quiet prayer,and every unexpected turn was teaching me how to live fully, how to stand still when the world shook, and how to carry gratitude and hope in equal measure. Faith held me through the unknown, through longing, through the contradictions that life placed in my path. It didn't demand that I choose one family over another. It asked that I be brave enough to seek the truth. When I finally searched for those who shared my first chapter, I realized that faith had never been about certainty. It had been about showing up, fully present, to every moment life gave me.

Looking back, I see now that the waiting, the searching, the quiet prayers, and the fear were leading me to the person I was meant to become. The faith I inherited taught me that stillness is not weakness, that patience is not passivity, and that courage is not the absence of fear but the choice to keep moving forward despite it. Life had been shaping me in ways I could not see. I have learned that the true measure of a life lived fully is not in the answers we find, but in the courage we summon to ask the questions and the grace with which we meet the unfolding of the story, even when it is not ours to control.

Chapter 15

When Dreams Fit

Inside a Knapsack

I used to believe that dreams had to be impressive to matter. They were bright, oversized things that demanded attention. The kind of dreams people pin to vision boards or speak about with the confidence of those who have always known where they came from and where they were going.

Mine were not like that.

My dreams were small enough to tuck away, modest enough to fold tightly, fragile enough that I guarded them. They lived zipped inside the knapsack I carried everywhere. Sometimes it was on my back, sometimes it was buried deep in the closet of my mind. These were dreams shaped by adoption, by the quiet ache of being lost, by a faith that flickered more often than it blazed.

Even before I understood language, I understood *absence*.
Adoption can offer roots, love, and stability. These are blessings I never take for granted but adoption also leaves a particular kind of shadow. A sense that the first chapter of your life was written in invisible ink.

Growing up, I could feel the shape of what I didn't know:
 the face of the woman who gave birth to me,
 the reason she let go,
 the story behind my first breath.

I could pretend I didn't care, but curiosity lived inside me like a dormant seed waiting for its spring.

My adoptive parents were good, loving, steadfast people. They were as steady as oak trees. I loved them deeply, and they gave me everything they could. But they couldn't answer the questions I was too ashamed or too scared to ask. So I learned to carry my wandering alone.

I didn't talk about it much, even to myself. Stillness became a hiding place.

If I stood still, maybe the feelings would settle.
If I stood still, maybe the ache would soften.
If I stood still long enough, maybe life would reveal answers without me having to go looking.

But life does what it does—*life happens, even when you stand still.*

The knapsack I carried as a child was made of faded green canvas, frayed at the corners and soft from use. At first it held snacks, then books, then the private scribbles of a boy trying to understand himself. It smelled faintly of pencil shavings and cut grass. When I picture it now, I imagine everything inside that wasn't physical. It included the dreams I was afraid to speak aloud, the belief that someone out there looked like me, and the hope that one day I'd feel whole.

Dreams don't stay dormant forever. They press against their own boundaries. As I grew older, the knapsack inside me became heavier. Each passing year added new questions, new hopes, and new unspoken grief.

Some days the weight felt ordinary. It was part of who I was. Other days, it felt impossibly heavy, and faith became the only thin thread connecting me to hope. Not faith in miracles or outcomes, but faith in the simple motion of life. Faith that forward was better than stuck, even when forward felt terrifying.

Still, for a long time, I stayed motionless.

I built a life. I had a routine. I had a version of myself that could function without knowing the truth of where I began. People saw a man who seemed solid, steady, and resilient. They didn't see the knapsack inside me, which was bulging with unanswered questions.

Sometimes life nudges you.
Sometimes it whispers.
And sometimes it cracks open the shell you've been hiding in.

My crack came quietly.

And then, without much warning, everything shifted. Deciding to look for my birth family felt like someone turning on a light in a room I had been living in my entire life. I didn't suddenly have all the answers, but I suddenly had faces, names, and histories that anchored me. In meeting them, I realized I hadn't been unproductive at all. My life had been quietly weaving two worlds, faith and identity, longing and belonging, so that when they finally met, I could step into the fullness of who I was meant to be.

The day everything began to change didn't announce itself with fireworks or revelation. It started quietly, the way most turning points do. I remember sitting with a piece of paper. It was just a name, a location, and a date but I felt the weight of it settle into my chest. It was small, almost insignificant to anyone else, but to me it felt like a key. A key to a door I had imagined for years but had never been brave enough to touch. For the first time, the questions in my heart had something to hold on to. Something real.

I told myself not to get ahead of things. One name didn't mean answers. One lead didn't guarantee a reunion. But even as I tried to be cautious, hope slipped in. It was gentle but persistent. It didn't roar. It whispered. And in that whisper was the feeling that maybe, just maybe, stillness had done its work. Maybe life had been moving beneath the surface the whole time, carrying me toward this moment while I stood wondering if anything would ever change.

As I began to search more deeply, I noticed a strange tug-of-war inside me that was clearly excitement braided with fear. I had longed for the truth for so long, but truth can be a dangerous thing. What if I wasn't wanted? What if I was forgotten? What if knowing where I came from didn't make me feel more whole, but instead opened a wound I didn't know how to tend? Faith steadied me in those moments, reminding me that answers don't promise comfort, but they do promise clarity. And I had reached a point in my life where clarity felt like salvation.

It was an ordinary afternoon. No drama. No thunderbolts. I was sitting at my kitchen table with a mug of cooling tea when the thought surfaced again: *I could look for them.*
This time it didn't slip away. It held me.

I didn't know how to begin. I wondered if they were even alive. There was a time when I questioned whether I had even come from a mother at all. My mind ran in circles. I was looking for the truth in the dark.

This time, I made a choice. I asked my good neighbor and friend, Rosemary Bachelor. I knew she had helped others find lost relatives. I asked her whether it was possible to find an adopted family.

"Yes," she said. "And I'll help you."

And so the waiting began. Every knock on my door made my heart race. As the days stretched on, fear crept in. The fear of finding nothing, the fear of finding too much, and the fear that the truth would be heavier than the wondering became a part of me each and every day.

What if I wasn't ready to search for opened doors?
What if it opened wounds instead?

Inside the knapsack of my chest, the dreams rustled again. Dreams rarely arrive with fireworks. They begin with a tug.

The search was slow, like wading through mud. Every quiet day without an answer invited my mind to invent its own stories. Stillness began to feel safer again. Maybe some stories were meant to stay sealed.

Then, one day, there was a knock at my door and it was Rosemary.

When our match was confirmed, I sat on the edge of my bed and cried. They were quiet tears from a place beyond words. I had imagined this moment all my life, but I never expected the relief that washed over me. It wasn't just finding my birth family. It was discovering proof that my story had roots.

She had spoken with a second cousin. He knew my name. He was willing to talk.

I'll never forget the piece of paper she held. It had simple handwriting with a single name, but those few words cracked something wide open.

My beginning had a name.

Something inside me that had been curled for decades unfolded. I broke down in tears, overwhelmed by relief, joy, and the deep sense that the long wait was finally over. At the same time, a new journey had just begun.

The first time I dialed a number connected to my past, my hands shook so badly I almost dropped the phone. It felt surreal, like I was trespassing into a story that wasn't entirely mine, even though the story had everything to do with me. The ring on the other end stretched into an eternity, each second echoing with the possibility of silence or rejection. But then a voice answered. It sounded familiar in a way that made no sense and yet all the sense in the world. I didn't introduce myself right away. I just listened, letting the sound settle into me like a memory waking up.

What followed was perfect. It was smooth. It was the fairy tale I used to imagine. It was real to me. There were pauses heavy with emotion, questions layered beneath every word, and a willingness on both sides to step into the unknown. And in that tender, trembling beginning, something inside me shifted. For the first time in my life, I felt the faint outline of belonging taking shape. It was not defined by answers yet, but by possibility.

And yet, even as this new world unfolded, I realized something unexpected: the search for identity doesn't end when an adoptee finds their birth family. It simply changes shape. Finding them didn't erase the journey. It expanded it. It gave me roots I had longed for, but also invited me to grow into a new understanding of myself. This one honored every chapter, every moment of stillness, every prayer whispered in the dark.

I had a wonderful conversation with my cousin and we talked for hours. He told me a little about himself and about my half-brothers and half-sisters. We agreed he would share my contact information with them so they could decide whether they wished to reach out. I knew I would be disappointed if none of them did, but I respected the possibility. I was stunned by how quickly everything was happening after waiting so long.

The cousin told me my mother had died of a heart attack at 58. He told me he had prepared a packet about me to send to my birth siblings so they could decide whether to pursue a connection. If they chose not to, that would be the end. I told myself that there would be no hard feelings.

The first person to contact me was my birth sister. She was open, warm, and friendly, and she made me feel as though I had known her all my life. My birth sister later admitted she was suspicious at first, fearing it might be a scam, but after speaking with me she let go of that worry.

Soon after, I received emails from one half-brother and two half-sisters, along with their contact information. I was so excited that I wrote back immediately. I shared information about myself, asked questions about my siblings, and asked about my birth mother. I also acknowledged the many feelings they might have had about learning of my existence. After all, I had unknowingly taken the place of their oldest brother. And I was struck by how humorous this family was. They had a similar humor that reminded me of my adoptive family.

My birth siblings and I exchanged messages. The messages were careful, emotional, and full of questions tucked beneath polite sentences. They told me they had no idea I existed. Our mother had never spoken of me. We were all stunned by the truth.

I told them about my loving adoptive parents and my adopted brother and sister.

My birth mother was not married at the time of my birth and was one of ten children. When I first met my half-siblings, they shared that they were not sure she even knew she had given birth to me due to her young age and the labor and delivery medications given at that time. If you expand on that story, there is a possibility that before she had fully recovered from the medications, I was taken from her and put into foster care.

My half-sister contacted my other siblings and arranged a family gathering later that summer. Everyone came except for the one brother who did not wish to meet me.

My half-siblings told me that my birth mother never talked about me to them ever, and like myself, they never even knew about me. No one is exactly sure what happened regarding my birth to this day. I'm not even sure if my mother, were she alive, could have told us. Even today there is a lot of mystery about my birth.

The information on the Non-Identifying Information Form I received from the State reported that my father was arrested on a morals charge because my mother was underage. My birth father was deceased when I learned of this. I wouldn't have gone near him anyway because I hated the thought about what he had done to my birth mother. To me, he had taken advantage of her, and I hated him for doing that.

Most of the family lives in Thetford, Vermont. Some live in New Hampshire and Maine. We know we cannot make up for the lost years, but we can move forward and share what comes as it comes. My two families have blended beautifully, and I am deeply grateful for that. They talk to each other even when I'm not involved. They check in on my health and arrange get-togethers on their own. There is nothing I cannot talk with them about.

I told each member of my biological family that I am gay because my parents taught me never to lie to people who matter. My adopted family has always known, even the younger ones, and I didn't want it to come out in a careless moment. I believe in being transparent with family.

One day, while sitting with Rosemary in her condo, she asked if I would like to see my mother's signature. I said yes, of course. Then she asked if I wanted to see a picture of my mother. With excitement and some trepidation, I said, "Oh yes, please."

I wasn't sure I was ready to see her after seventy-one years of waiting. When I saw her photograph, I began to smile. She looked like me. She smiled like me. Tears streamed down my cheeks. I didn't know what to say.

Before the COVID-19 pandemic, my relationship with my birth half-siblings grew stronger. When the pandemic hit, I was confined to my apartment except on special occasions. I couldn't see them in person at all. Thank goodness for technology. Cell phones and FaceTime allowed us to stay connected. I asked countless questions over the phone, building bonds from afar. Love and support grew throughout that difficult time.

It was also almost more than I could bear. I had finally found my birth siblings after seventy-plus years and then hadn't been able to see them. There were times I broke down and cried uncontrollably. They became wonderfully stabilizing people in my life. For that, I will be eternally grateful.

I wondered what my parents would think if they knew I had found my birth mother. I believe they would have been happy for me. They always supported everything I wanted to pursue. I wondered, too, what my adopted siblings might have thought. I will never know how my adopted brother, Larry, would have felt, since he passed away before I could share my new information with him. But I do know how my adopted sister, Rachel, felt. She told me before she died that she was very happy for me. Rachel and my birth family even met over a wonderful meal at my birth sister's home a couple of summers ago. I only wish Rachel had had a more positive experience when finding her own birth mother and birth sister. When she found them, it didn't go as well as it did for me. I felt sad for her and wished I could have made it better in some way.

I feel fortunate to have met my birth family and to see how well they have blended with my adopted family. Without them, my life would have continued with a deep hole I never expected to be filled. That dream might never have been, had I not called my cousin Kenneth that day.

In the days that followed, I felt raw. I was flooded by information. Looking back, I might have taken things slower, in smaller pieces. But life doesn't always unfold in tidy sequences.

I also never got to say anything to my birth mother in her entire lifetime. I never even got to say goodbye because she died before I met her. Sitting here now, I am crying because I realize how little closure I had with so many important people in my life. Perhaps I denied that truth for years as a way to protect myself.

When I stood face-to-face with the people whose blood ran through my veins, I understood something I had never known: belonging can lie dormant, waiting years to be awakened.

I saw pieces of myself in their smiles, in the way they held my hands, in the way their eyes softened at the sight of me. I saw the beginning of my story.

Finding my birth family didn't erase the complications of adoption. It didn't replace the parents who raised me or diminish the love they poured into my life. But it gave shape to the emptiness. It gave color to the blurred lines. It gave me a fuller map.

Now, when I think of that knapsack, I imagine opening it and seeing everything I carried for so long: fear, longing, hope, faith and dreams. Not grand dreams, but meaningful ones. The kind that fit inside a knapsack because they were never meant to impress. They were meant to guide.

Finding my birth family didn't complete me. It expanded me. It stretched my heart in ways I didn't know were possible. It allowed me to stand still without feeling stuck, to move without fear.

About six years ago, on a gray fall day, my friend Rosemary took me to the cemetery in Thetford, Vermont, where my mother is buried. We found her grave, and at the time it felt like enough. But today, sitting alone with two photographs of her that my half-sister sent me, it no longer feels like enough. Maybe it never will. I feel robbed because I will never be able to ask my mother if she was happy, or how she felt about her life, or what she imagined it might have been like had she known about me. I cannot ask the million questions a son longs to ask. And she will never get to ask me anything in return. I believe in the hereafter, so perhaps I will simply have to wait for that day.

I once believed faith was the opposite of uncertainty, but during the long months of searching for my birth family, I learned otherwise. Faith wasn't the light cutting through the fog. It was choosing to keep walking even when the path was hidden. In that stillness between steps, I discovered the quiet truth at the center of my story: **life happens even when you stand still**. The fog taught me things clarity never had. Identity isn't a destination but a process. And by the time I finally met the people whose faces I had imagined for decades, I understood how much that slow unfolding had prepared me.

Some realizations arrive like confessions. They are unexpected, heavy, and true. Hearing my birth mother's name for the first time was one of those moments. It felt as though a locked door had opened inside me, and for a breathless second, I understood that my life had been moving toward that moment all along. I had spent years feeling like a misplaced puzzle piece, and suddenly the picture sharpened. Even in all the years I felt frozen or lost, the story was moving; **life was happening even when I stood still**, stitching itself together beneath the surface.

The knapsack is lighter now.
Not because my journey is finished. Stories like mine rarely tie themselves into neat bows. Because I finally dared to unpack the dreams I had carried for so long, I learned the lesson this journey kept trying to teach me. Sometimes standing still is not the absence of movement, but the space where healing finally catches up.

What I found inside was not just a family.
Not just answers.
I found myself while **life happens, even
when you stand still**. Somehow, life carries
you exactly where you need to go.

REFERENCES

Austin, Wyeth. "Spirituality vs Religion-a Deep Analysis." Medium, Thoughts And Ideas, 30 Mar. 2021, medium.com/indian-thoughts/spirituality-vs-religion-a-deep-analysis-f0b884147314.

Healthcare, GE. "Atrial Fibrillation: Knowing the Basics." Clinical View, 22 Aug. 2025, clinicalview.gehealthcare.com/white-paper/atrial-fibrillation-knowing-basics?utm_medium=cpc&utm_source=google&utm_campaign=USC-USC-PCS-ALL-AlwaysOn-COV-SC-25-01&utm_term=&utm_content=18727281303&npclid=Cj0KCQjwqqDFBhDhARIsAIHTIkuESLrE1OeoAEYgzJpHYyDsyJ6KeaNZoe4AExxRm56lllHtSrsjVqcaAr4BEALw_wcB&gad_source=1&gad_campaignid=18727281303&gbraid=0AAAAABn7i5X-Kti8AJIfaH5VL03MWPpiQ&gclid=Cj0KCQjwqqDFBhDhARIsAIHTIkuESLrE1OeoAEYgzJpHYyDsyJ6KeaNZoe4AExxRm56lllHtSrsjVqcaAr4BEALw_wcB.

Chat GPT (AI) assisted in some of the quotes in this book and assisted with grammatical editing.

"Ptosis (Droopy Eyelid)." Cleveland Clinic, 1 July 2025, my.clevelandclinic.org/health/diseases/14418-ptosis-droopy-eyelid.

"Rickets." Mayo Clinic, Mayo Foundation for Medical Education and Research, 25 Apr. 2025,www.mayoclinic.org/diseases-conditions/rickets/symptoms-causes/syc-20351943.

"Sadomasochism." Encyclopædia Britannica, Encyclopædia Britannica, inc., 31 July 2025, www.britannica.com/topic/sadomasochism.

What is water intoxication?. Cleveland Clinic. (2025, November 18). https://my.clevelandclinic.org/health/diseases/water-intoxication

www.ingramcontent.com/pod-product-compliance
Lightning Source LLC
Chambersburg PA
CBHW070656130626
46553CB00005B/1725